Conversations

Other Luce Irigaray titles available from Continuum:

Democracy Begins Between Two
The Ethics of Sexual Difference
Luce Irigaray: Key Writings
Thinking the Difference
To Speak is Never Neutral
The Way of Love
Luce Irigaray: Teaching
Sharing the World

Conversations

Luce Irigaray

with

Stephen Pluháček and Heidi Bostic, Judith Still,
Michael Stone, Andrea Wheeler, Gillian Howie,
Margaret R. Miles and Laine M. Harrington,
Helen A. Fielding, Elizabeth Grosz,
Michael Worton, Birgitte H. Midttun

continuum

Continuum
The Tower Building, 11 York Road, London SE1 7NX
80 Maiden Lane, Suite 704, New York NY 10038

www.continuumbooks.com

British Library Cataloguing-in-Publication Data
A catalogue record for this book is available from the British Library.

ISBN: HB: 1-8470-6035-8
978-1-8470-6035-8
PB: 1-8470-6036-6
978-1-8470-6036-5

Library of Congress Cataloguing-in-Publication Data
A catalog record for this book is available from the Library of Congress.

Designed and typeset by Kenneth Burnley, Wirral, Cheshire
Printed and bound in Great Britain by Athenaeum Press Ltd, Gateshead, Tyne and Wear

Contents

Acknowledgements

I would like to express my gratitude to all the participants who devoted time to prepare questions to ask me, especially to those who did so in order to better pass on my thought either in their teaching or in their writing essays. I am also grateful to Angelika Dickmann for helping me to collect the final electronic material of the book and to prepare it for publication.

I would like to thank all the editors and publishers for their kind permission to reproduce the original, slightly amended or partial versions of these conversations: in particular, Springer Science and Business Media for the conversation with Stephen Pluháček and Heidi Bostic (originally published as 'Thinking life as relation', *Man and World* 29/4 [1996]: 343–60) and a part of the conversation with Helen Fielding (published with the translation of my essay on Maurice Merleau-Ponty 'To paint the invisible', *Continental Philosophy* 37/4 [2004]: 389–405); the editorial board of *Nottingham French Studies* for the conversation with Judith Still (originally published as 'Towards a wisdom of love: Dialogue between Luce Irigaray and Judith Still around *Dialogues* and *The Way of Love* at the ICA 16 December 2002', *Nottingham French Studies* 42/2 [2003]: 142–51); the editors of the *Journal of Romance Studies* for the conversation with Andrea Wheeler (originally published as 'About being-two in an architectural perspective: Interview with Luce Irigaray', *Journal of Romance Studies* 4/2 [2004], 91–107); the editors Stacy Gillis, Gillian Howie and Rebecca Muford and the publisher Palgrave Macmillan for the conversation with Gillian Howie (originally published as 'Interview with Luce Irigaray', in *Third Wave Feminism: A Critical Exploration* [expanded 2nd edn; Basingstoke: Palgrave Macmillan, 2007], pp. 283–91).

Many thanks also to Birgitte H. Midttun for permission to include in this collection the English version of an interview that she had with me for her forthcoming book in Norwegian, to be published by Humanist: *Kvinnereisen – 10 møter med feminismens tenkere* (*Woman's Journeys: Meetings with Feminist Thinkers*).

Introduction

Dialogue has always been a way of approaching knowledge and truth. Depending on the tradition and the era, one person or the other asks questions. Sometimes it is the master who questions the disciples in order to guide them, and sometimes it is the disciples who question the master in order to learn, at least when they dare to do that and the master agrees to participate in such an exchange. Our times, unfortunately, rather privilege criticism and arrogance, and questioning often amounts today to putting the master on probation instead of being a quest for truth. What is more, as it is generally believed that wondering about something presupposes a certain ignorance, it is no longer in one's own name that one asks questions but in the name of those whom one teaches or whom one is presumed to represent and who are supposed to be ignorant. Foremost in this regard are journalists, who ask questions in order to inform others without taking any part themselves in the conversation. Only neutrality with respect to the truth at stake but also between the interviewer and the interviewee would be acceptable and would correspond to the ethics of a good interview.

Thus, the main concern is no longer to reach the truth, a concern for which dialogue would be the most appropriate method, and, furthermore, it is no longer even to have a dialogue, because the questions are not asked in the name of the one who takes part in the conversation. Only a technical competence in carrying out an interview remains, in which criticism and conflict are indispensable to sustain interest and, thus, the attention of the audience. Asepsis alone is acceptable and an absolute relativism, with the exception of obedience to fashionable leanings and political correctness, which can vary according to the media, environments, countries and cultures.

This way of holding a conversation has invaded intellectual circles. It is presumed to be the only way of guaranteeing the scientific nature of conversation. And the more this loses any content, the more the formalism of the process, which ought to convey that content, becomes the unique guarantee of a supposed truth. In fact, conversation then takes place between two persons who do not know one another, who do not share anything and who behave towards one another as robots, separated by a sort of isolating closure or a mediating third possibly still more impersonal and indifferent – except where money is concerned.

One could send the supposed defenders of these norms in relating to truth back to the dialogues of Plato – why not to the *Symposium*? – in order that they might inform themselves about the manner in which these dialogues infolded. They could then discover that love was approached in a context of love affairs between the participants, who were almost somehow making love. Truth was then perhaps more true than the truth claimed by our contemporaries, because it was based on experience. A personal experience, which involves our flesh itself instead of taking place almost *in vitro* through sanitized methods. An experience that, henceforth, would soil the truth of ourselves so much that we ought to give it up.

The conversations which are gathered here do not obey such imperatives, which are programmed by what is most questionable and futile in the effects of our metaphysical tradition. The persons taking part in these conversations for the most part know one another, and they talk to one another without renouncing either their bodily and sensible belonging or their convictions. If the exchanges are not yet fully dialogues, it is because the participants are not at the same stage of their journeys, have not lived through the same experiences nor produced the same work. It is also this way because the framework of these conversations is, more or less explicitly, questioning my own work, a work in which the questioners take an interest and to which they devote a part of their own research. Reciprocity in the exchanges was thus not really always possible, but my answers aim at such an outcome both with regard to the participants in the exchanges and to every reader of the book.

Unfortunately, most of us have stopped believing in a supra-sensible truth that exists outside of ourselves and would be valid for all people in all spaces and times. Now truth results from who or what we are, from our experience(s), from our journey, among other things from our advancement in the recognition of the other as other and in our ability to exchange with such an other in mind. The quality of the conversations, which are gathered in this book, could be assessed, not according to the degree of asepsis and disengagement, but according to the degree of attentive respect for the other. That is, according to the involvement of the persons who enter into dialogue in the exchange itself; instead of their neutralization for the benefit of a truth indifferent to the one and the other, a truth that they would attempt to reach in the name of a scientific ascetism beyond any personal involvement. No doubt, something of this ideal remains, especially on the part of certain participants. Taking time to reflect about oneself is not yet, or no longer, the habit of cultural circles, who are ready to object to you that Plato offers a model of dialogue between philosophers, without noting how much the participants in the *Symposium* threw themselves into their search of truth. For these Greeks, truth was not yet the outcome of a mere logical reasoning. The relation between themselves and argumentation was still at work and alive in the discovery of truth, even if they aim more and more to substitute the *logos* itself for it. But it is still starting from their experience that Socrates and his disciples talk about love. Only between men, it is true! Undeniably, Socrates mentions the words of Diotima, but in her absence. There is thus no exchange in difference between the sexes or genders in the *Symposium*. Socrates talks in the name of Diotima, but not with her. The way to enter into dialogue between man and woman is thus lacking in this presumed model of dialogue. And this spoils not only the content of the words, but also their logical organization, with a lack prejudicial to truth itself. Our Western tradition has suffered and still suffers because of such a lack, which notably appears in its claim to aim at a neutral and sterile truth as the very best for humanity. It has also missed a correct conception of what gender itself is, for which, and already in the words of Diotima, it substituted generation, preventing in this way a possible dialogue, especially a dialogue both amorous and about love.

In fact, a dialogue always ought to correspond to a love story, if not between the two persons who enter into dialogue, at least between them and that about which they try to exchange. The best dialogues happen when love exists both between the two persons and towards the subject which is at stake between them. Such a situation still existed in the time in which Socrates lived, but it was vanishing because ideas or ideals began to replace life itself, and love that life needs to rest and develop. Which was also questioned by the absence of Diotima: even if Socrates appealed to her advice on the subject, she is kept out of the symposium. How can views of love have any worth outside of any practice of love itself? And what part of life, of love and truth is left to one side when relations stop at relations between those who are alike? How then to maintain the two? To preserve this two from being immersed in the multiple? From falling back into undifferentiation? No doubt some features distinguish those who are the same at a sexuate level, but that often blind attraction determined by sexuate difference no longer exists between them, an attraction which often becomes destructive for lack of cultivation of its transcendental dimension. A transcendence, then, which not only stays beyond and outside ourselves and to which we ought to submit our desire, but rather that the desire for the different other can awaken in ourselves.

A dialogue always ought to take place between two people awakened in this way, who question themselves in order to guide one another on the path towards coming closer in respect for their differences and transcendences. Who also question how they could create between them a shareable world: a truth, an art, an ethics and a politics, which transcend each one but which they could both share. Then the questioner and the responder really exist and can alternately exchange their roles. And the questions have a content concerning a truth both external and internal to each subject, a truth both objective and subjective, which asks questions about being – and Being – of each one and their own world, as well as about a world in which all humans could dwell and share between them.

Exchange, then, is real and not formal, and because it has to do with reality between two humans, it passes on a truth that somehow is shareable by others. This is the intention which animates the conversations gathered here. They touch on various cultural fields and cultures, and took place at different times. After some hesitation, I decided to present them in chronological order because it is the order which most corresponds to the reality and the truth. I hope that my academic questioners will forgive me for daring to propose as a postscript an interview with a journalist. I thought that to compare this interview with the other conversations could be relaxing and instructive, because the journalist asks questions that academics do not pose, but about which many people wonder.

Luce Irigaray, October 2007

Thinking Life as Relation

Conversation between

Luce Irigaray, Stephen Pluháček
and Heidi Bostic

Stephen Pluháček and Heidi Bostic: We met Luce Irigaray in Paris in the spring of 1996 while attending her seminar, 'La question de l'autre', at the École des Hautes Études en Sciences Sociales. Our discussions there focused on her recent work, including *I Love to You*, *Je, tu, nous* and *Thinking the Difference*, which constitutes the basis of this interview. The following questions were presented in written form and were responded to in writing. During numerous meetings, the questions and responses were discussed and analysed. In this manner, from May to August 1996, the following interview came about. We wish to thank Luce Irigaray for her patience and insight throughout this process.

*　　*　　*

STEPHEN PLUHÁČEK and HEIDI BOSTIC: Your work, like the work of certain other contemporary philosophers, puts the universal subject into question. But unlike many other philosophers, you seem more able to offer, and more open to the idea of, concrete alternatives and concrete plans of action for effecting changes inside the space opened by the resituation of the universal subject. How is it that you are able to propose positive and concrete alternatives and plans of action?

LUCE IRIGARAY: Do I dare say that perhaps my way of questioning a universal subject is right and that, as such, it permits, and even demands both a theoretical and practical refounding of culture?

So, I do not believe that to question the universal subject starting from the multiple is sufficient, because the multiple can always be equivalent to a multiple or a sub-multiple of *one*. The explicit or implicit measure remains the *one*, more or less real, imaginary or simply mathematical. The critique of the universal subject cannot be limited to the substitution of the multiple for the one because it deconstructs certain values necessary for subjective constitution without a questioning radical enough to permit the emergence of other values. Thus, to deconstruct all reference to unity, to the absolute, to the ideal, to the transcendence and so on, without bringing about a reorganization of the energy invested in such values risks the disintegration of the subject to the benefit of the savage reign of death drives or of the coming to power of an even more totalitarian authority, these two possibilities not being incompatible.

The gesture that I make is different, probably because I start from reality, from a universal reality: sexual difference. The deconstruction of the *one* generally realizes itself either through abstract models or through non-universal empirical realities, in space and time: the putting into question is therefore too partial to reach a real universal. Moreover, this deconstruction often is fulfilled in an auto-logical manner, as for the construction of the *one*. It is therefore the latter, which finds itself, eventually passed from the real to the imaginary or reduced in a simple numerology.

In order to question the universal subject, it is necessary to approach another logic. The only logic that can assure a rational and universal foundation is that which starts from the reality of two genders, masculine and feminine. Such a logic compels us to rethink, theoretically and practically, the subjective constitution as well as the one of the individual or collective world. The *one* no longer remains here the visible or invisible, conscious or unconscious paradigm, which governs rational organization; this organization henceforth takes into consideration the existence of two subjects, irreducible one to the other.

Certainly, this reality of the *two* has always existed. But it was submitted to the imperatives of a logic of the *one*, the *two* being reduced then to a pair of opposites not independent one from the other. Moreover, the duality was subordinated to a genealogical order, a hierarchical order, in space and in time, which prevented considering the necessity of the passage to another mode of thinking, and of living.

My procedure consists therefore in substituting, for a universal constructed of taking account of only one part of reality, a universal, which respects the totality of the real. The universal therefore is no longer *one* nor unique, it is *two*. This obliges us to refound our culture, our societies in order to reach a civilization at the same time more real, more just, and more universal.

S.P. and H.B.: You have suggested that a critique of patriarchy, which is not accompanied by the definition of new values founded on natural reality, runs the risk of being nihilistic. What is this natural reality and what does it mean for a critique of patriarchy to be accompanied by the definition of new values founded on this natural reality?

Epistemologically speaking, how may one gain access to this natural reality?

L.I.: This question rejoins the one which precedes, and permits the completion of its response. A pertinent critique of patriarchy implies an interpretation of its system as insufficient in order to render account of one part of the real. Without returning to a real more real or more total, the inversion of an order of values is nihilistic in the bad sense of the term.

For me, questioning the patriarchal world has been possible from the discovery of the fabricated character of my feminine identity. Neither my consciousness nor even my body had free access to the real. I could not pass from nature to the spiritual because I was held in a determination of the one and of the other which was foreign to me. The sensible as well as the intelligible were presented to me and imposed upon me according to norms which were not proper to me. Therefore, I had to recover an immediate perception of the real and at the same time to elaborate a symbolic universe which corresponded to it.

Let us take an example. If my body, as feminine, was reduced to a nature for man, indeed for humanity, it can not at all be the nature from which I perceive the world, I perceive myself, and I can be and become subjectively and objectively that which I really am. If my woman's nature was considered as living matter at the service of the other's desire and of reproduction, I could not experience it as a 'for me' and assume its becoming spiritual through a dialectic of in-self and for-self. It was necessary therefore to come back to a relation with nature which was not already artificially structured. It is moreover partially starting from a strangeness of my immediate sensible experience to these values that I began to interrogate the patriarchal universe.

But I live in a cultural tradition. My relation to the world, to others, and to myself is marked by it. I had to, I still have to, effect a gesture that is at least double: deconstruct the basic elements of the culture which alienate me and discover the symbolic norms which can at the same time preserve the singularity of my nature and permit me to elaborate its culture.

This enterprise is not simple! It requires an aptitude to perceive and to analyse perceptions, about which the tradition of India, in particular that of yoga, has taught me much. Vigilance in relations to the other has equally alerted me to a necessary respect for the difference between the other and me. The consideration of dominant values and their being put in perspective in the unfolding of History has allowed me to relativize the cultural universe in which I was living. And the analysis of the discourse of philosophers has revealed to me that the argumentation internal to their system often necessitates bids for power or jumps which bear witness to the partially artificial character of the logic which is at work here. These are only some examples of epistemological recourses used for questioning a cultural horizon.

S.P. and H.B.: You have indicated that a cosmic or natural order exists which could and should serve as the basis for a terrestrial order – social or political. Why and how should the terrestrial order be based upon the cosmic order? Furthermore, if men are less linked than women to cosmic rhythms, why should they conform to these rhythms?

L.I.: I don't understand what you mean by 'serve as the basis'. If you signify that it is necessary to start from the micro- and from the macro-cosm to organize a social and political order, then I can recognize in your question a dimension which is important to me. A social and political order which is not founded upon the real is precarious, and even dangerous. All the imaginary disturbances, all the authoritarian deviations, all the cultural regressions are possible here.

I don't think however that it suffices to start from the cosmic or natural order to build a social or political order. This would risk falling again into the errors of the patriarchal world. In my opinion, a harmonious civil community, an accomplished democracy can only be founded upon relations between citizens. But these relations must be at the same time respectful of the needs and desires of each person, and be as non-hierarchical as possible, nevertheless assuring the cohesion of the society. In this sense, a relation between a man and a woman both capable of transforming their immediate attraction into civil coexistence seems to me a valid base for a social and political order. Of course, it is necessary to multiply this relation between two as many times as there exists an encounter between two citizens of different genders. But the human community is woven right through by such encounters. It is therefore possible to constitute it starting from this relational place or bond.

The social order is thus constructed in the respect for nature and for its cultural elaboration, necessary for elevating the relation between the genders to a civil level. That woman lives in greater continuity with the cosmos does not exempt her from elaborating this dimension of herself in order to be capable of a civil relation with man. It is in this sense that I have spoken of a necessary proof of negativity, for her, in the relation to the other. That said, it is possible to hope that her proximity to the micro- and to the macro-cosm lends her to be a better guardian of the safety of nature than man has been up until the present. Planet Earth and the world of the living certainly are in need of it!

S.P. and H.B.: In *Je, tu, nous*, you write that the rapport between biology and culture has not been sufficiently examined, and that despite the fact that biology has been used to exploit women, they should not avoid (re)thinking this relation between biology and culture. Given the possibility that this (re)thinking of the biology/culture relation could lead to a new and greater exploitation of women, what are your suggestions about how to (re)think this relation? ('The Culture of Difference', in *Je, tu, nous*, p. 46).

L.I.: Obviously, I do not agree with the expression used by Freud in reference to the feminine condition, 'Anatomy is destiny'. The use made of it is at once authoritarian, final and devalorizing for woman.

But what has served to exploit women is a biology interpreted in terms more masculine than feminine. In the chapter 'On the maternal order', which precedes the passage to which you allude, a woman biologist objects to the patriarchal argument concerning the necessity of the paternal law in order to break off the mother–infant fusion since, in the very womb of the mother, nature has planned a third, the placenta, between the mother and the foetus.

This revelation can only contribute to the awareness of women in view of their liberation from laws imposed upon them from the outside. It invites them, on the other hand, to respect that much better a distance and a difference with the other that nature, in themselves, respects already. No male biologist has expressed in these terms, to my knowledge, the role of the placenta as regulating third. Why? Would it not be, among other reasons, because it is a question there of a biology of the relation between two living human beings? Which corresponds little to a masculine anatomic science, usually thought starting from cadavers or from animal experimentation.

This same tendency is found moreover in other scientific processes realized by men. Whether it is a matter of biology, physics, mathematics, linguistics, logic, psychology, etc., generally the closed, the finite, the 'dead', the isolated is preferred to the open, the in-finite, the living, the relation. Sometimes there exists a play of oppositions between extremes but it is only belatedly, marginally and not without resistances that science has become interested in 'the partly-opened', in the 'permeability of membranes', in the theory of 'fields', in the 'dynamic of fluids', in the current programming of discourse, in the 'dialogic', etc. Now these objectives have more affinity with the feminine universe.

It cannot be harmful to a woman to discover the reality of her biological economy. What harms her is to be subjected to a science which is not appropriate for her, or to be reduced to a simple nature. To be opposed to a knowledge of nature in order that this not be used to harm women, would not be an homage to them. On the other hand, it is useful to incite women to vigilance about what does or does not correspond to them. It is also important that they not accept being reduced to a pure body, a pure nature, whether it be by inertia or by submission to the other. As I said in 'Your Health: What, or Who, Is It?', what allows women to escape diverse forms of illness, physical and mental, is their own desire, their own will, their own access to the spiritual world, their breath, their 'soul'.

S.P. and H.B.: To what degree does the effort to rethink the relation between biology and culture remain insufficient in so far as it fails to take into consideration other species? That is to say, is maternity limited to the production of children within one species? Whereas the relation mother/placenta/child plays a more or less important role in a social imaginary, are there not similar and perhaps more important relations which are established not only among organisms of the same species, but also among different species, as is the case with microorganisms (for example, certain types of bacteria) on which human life depends and who also depend upon humans for survival? In this direction, could you imagine a motherhood which is open to men as well as to women?

L.I.: I do not have enough knowledge to reply exhaustively to this question. I think I have partially answered it in the preceding and following responses. It seems to me that the questioning turns on an antecedent, or perhaps a future, of the life animated by consciousness. It is thus that I would designate approximately the human child: capable of autonomy became capable of consciousness. I am not in a position to elucidate such perspectives, which are partially imaginary.

Shifting the question a little – not so much really – I could say that, to live maternity, men should accomplish two cultural revolutions: to prefer life over death, to be capable of a radical respect for the other's alterity. Without these two mutations, I think that men are not capable of engendering the living endowed with autonomous existence with respect to them. Is it not thus that maternity can be described?

I would also ask: why the will to be a 'mother' rather than to assume an identity of man, of father in the respect of one's limits? It is thanks to gender difference that another human is engendered. What will result from the blurring of identities? Whom and what does this serve today? To surpass a still unaccomplished human destiny? Why this immoderation? Is it not, once again, a vehicle of death more than of life?

S.P. and H.B.: In your work, you often refer to a natural reality said to be living. Could you indicate how and where the line is established between the living and the non-living? Additionally, how is the establishment of this line linked to gender?

L.I.: I have much reflected on this question. I think that it is close to the one on the possible engendering of the living by man in himself, on the maternal model. I am not sure that I have finished my meditations on the problem! Today, I would say that the living is that which continues to grow, to become. This growth cannot be reduced, in any way, to a proliferation of the same, to its multiplication nor to its simple repetition as happens in certain physical or mental illnesses. It implies a constant relation between the same and the different, in which is assimilated from the different only that which does not destroy the organism of the same nor that of the other. Willing only the same or only the different destroys life. Frequenting only the same or only the different represents a danger for the metabolism of life. To these considerations, it is of course fitting to add the problems relative to belonging to a species – human, for example – to a kingdom – vegetable, for example.

The existence of gender within the human species is certainly a factor protective of the living because it maintains a necessary economy in the relations between the same and the different. It is interesting to note that the manifestation of gender is assured by particular chromosomes, different in women and in men, whose effect is not exclusively somatic. The safeguarding of life would be in some way dependent on chromosomes not reducible to a purely corporeal genetics. Which can incite us to meditate on our desires for immortality, for eternity, for incorporeal divinities!

S.P. and H.B.: We will turn now towards linguistics. You are a philosopher who also employs linguistic tools. According to you, what is the relation between philosophy and linguistics? What can each discipline offer to the other?

L.I.: No one will deny that philosophy is constructed with language. In the West, this discipline has often been called metaphysics, that is to say a science capable of organizing material or immediately sensible realities with logical instruments which removed them from their first nature. The birth of Western philosophy is accompanied by the constitution of a *logos*, a language obeying rules such as those of self-identity, of non-contradiction, and so on, which distinguish it from a simple empirical language. These logical rules have been defined in order to ensnare the totality of the real in the nets of language, and thus to remove it from sensible experience, from the ever in-finite contiguity of daily life.

Philosophy thus represents an artificially constructed language in comparison to what is called natural language. But the latter is itself already constructed and there is an interaction between philosophical discourse and everyday discourse.

The experience of linguistics taught me to reflect on the production of language more than most other philosophers do. This led me to question the linguistic instrument supposed capable of discovering, articulating and transmitting the truth. I realized at least two things which seem decisive to me. First, the language that philosophy uses is not, in itself, neuter: it is marked by a gender, notably grammatical, which in a way does not correspond to reality. Philosophy cannot therefore claim universal truth if it uses such a language without interpreting it; philosophy appears as a partial truth and, in some way, as dogmatic because it imposes as true that which corresponds to the truth of a certain subject blind to its singularities. A single gender marks philosophical discourse in its form, its content, the definition of the subject, the relation to the world, the limits of the horizon.

Now, there exist two subjects, irreducible one to the other. My linguistic training enabled me to verify it scientifically. Man and woman do not speak in the same way, do not structure the relation between matter or nature and mind in a similar manner. The reflection on discourse, on language, to which I was led through an education in linguistics, enabled me to interpret the history of Western philosophy, to interrogate the particularities of its truth and its lacks. One of these is particularly evident: the small number of logical means that the masculine subject has developed for communicating in the present with another subject different from him, in particular with a subject of another gender. Analysis of feminine discourse shows that the woman is much more attentive to this than the man. But she lacks logical rules in order to be able to realize this tendency in the respect for herself and for the other. Reflecting on language produced by the two genders can provide thoughts about the subjective and objective transformations necessary for a perspective appropriate to the feminine subject and for intercommunication between the genders.

S.P. and H.B.: Your work often seems phenomenological and dialectical at the same time. How do you characterize your method?

L.I.: I don't think it is possible to speak of one single method. Criticizing and constructing necessitate different procedures. Moreover, my manner of criticizing is new because it has recourse to interpretation more than to simple judgment. And, in order to interpret, I use several ways, such as discourse analysis, putting into historical perspective, inversion, etc. But, I often use these procedures differently than in the past. Thus, with regard to inversion, as I explained it in *I Love to You*, I 'inverse' myself as much if not more than I 'inverse' others, the theory of others. To leave the patriarchal horizon required, on my part, a certain turning over of my subjectivity, the access to an autonomous perspective, an autonomous look, beginning from which I was able to perceive from an outside the cultural world which surrounded me.

This radical turning over of an immediate point of view, including on the intellectual level, required nevertheless some dialectical articulations with the past and the future of the History in which I am situated. It also demanded a faithfulness to experience and rigour in its phenomenological elaboration. A certain recourse, or return, to the phenomenological method seems necessary in order to make enter into the universe of our rationality some natural, corporeal, sensible realities which until now had been removed from it. It is true for me. In considering the unfolding of the history of philosophy, it seems that it is the same way for other philosophers.

Using phenomenology without dialectic would risk nevertheless a reconstruction of a solipsistic world, including a feminine world unconcerned with the masculine world or which accepts remaining parallel to the latter. The dialectical method, such as I use it, is not at the service of the reassumption (*Aufhebung*) of all singularity into an absolute objectivity to be shared by any subject. My way uses the negative as a path which permits, at each moment, dialogue between subjects in the respect of singularities, in particular of gender. Here, the negative is therefore insurmountable and the absolute can never be unique nor universally shared. The negative maintains real and living the *dialegomai* between subjectivities which, beyond appearing to self and to the other, must speak to one another in order to be and to become self, in order to elaborate a culture resulting from the spiritual fecundity of subjective differences.

S.P. and H.B.: In a woman, how can one separate the characteristics resulting from her sociocultural oppression, and the characteristics which reflect, so to speak, her 'being'?

L.I.: It is important to distinguish characteristics of the oppression already codified in the culture and those that the woman continues to create herself each day. Both suppose a hierarchy between the genders. For example, the linguistic practices which unequally value that which is related to the masculine gender and to the feminine gender are a mark of oppression; they can appear at the level of gender properly speaking, of connotations of words or of representations. It is the same for religious values and, more generally, symbolic values which are already instituted. Social inequalities take place in a cultural context which makes them possible thanks to an ideology.

The socio-cultural world is not, in itself, non-egalitarian, but a sexist worldvision permits it to be that way. Now such a view is still very much alive, both in cultural stereotypes and in the way in which women perpetuate them each day through their behaviour. Everyday experiences demonstrate that women have more respect for the speech of men, that they listen better to them, and more willingly have confidence in them. Already, the mother attends to the will of the little boy more than to that of the little girl. Even if her behaviour is inspired by desire, it is important to modify it in order to not maintain a devaluing ideology towards the feminine subject.

In addition to these values and behaviours to be modified, there are others, little known, still to be discovered and cultivated in order to affirm the existence of feminine identity. Thus, experiences in mixed groups of different cultures, languages, ages, sociocultural membership show that women privilege in their speaking intersubjectivity, the relation to the other gender, the relation between two, men preferring the subject–object relation, the relation to the same gender, and that between the one and a little-differentiated many: the people, the society, the citizens. It doesn't appear desirable to abandon the spontaneous choices of women. They have an obvious value and cannot be considered as inferior to the choices of men. But, it is necessary to cultivate them. So, the preference for the relation with the other gender, peculiar to the existence and to the being of the woman, must be practiced neither as a subjection nor to the detriment of the dialogue with one's own gender.

S.P. and H.B.: In *An Ethics of Sexual Difference*, one finds the description of two sorts of feminine relationships. The one, horizontal, is linked to the relation between women and between sisters. The other, vertical, is linked to the relation between daughter and mother, mother and daughter. What can we do to ensure that a vertical relation does not become hierarchical?

L.I.: The verticality of the relation between daughter and mother is linked to nature. It implies a complicity in belonging to the same nature and also the possibility of *doing as*: begetting in oneself, nurturing . . . The verticality of the relation to the mother cannot be thought, according to me, like the relation to the father, *a fortiori* to the God as Father. It is inscription in genealogy, in the unfolding of the history of the human species as life. Certainly it is fitting to raise the mother–daughter relation to a cultural dimension. This requires taking up and developing elements of civilization that we find, for instance, in archaic Greece, in Middle- and Far-Eastern traditions. The culture of the filiation with the mother will remain much more tied to nature than that of filiation with the father. Even on the spiritual level, it preserves a relation to macro- or micro-cosmic reality, it remains in continuity with matter.

The rupture with the natural universe intervenes, for woman, more in the horizontal relation. Being capable of human relations with other women, with sisters, demands, from her, being able to overcome her instincts, her submission to nature, her fusion with or adherence to another body. Spiritual conquest, for the feminine gender, goes through what I call 'virginity', that is to say the opening of a transcendental space in the relation to self and to the other. This meaning of the word 'virgin' is to be distinguished then from the assimilation of virginity to the conservation or non-conservation of a corporeal hymen. It is a question of a becoming spiritual, aiming at the maintenance of the integrity of the self and of the other in proper becoming (*le devenir propre*) and in common becoming (*le devenir commun*).

S.P. and H.B.: In realizing a critique of the traditional concept of identity, you speak of 'relational identity'. Could you explain what this relational identity is, and how it differs from the traditional concept of identity?

L.I.: According to the traditional logic, identity refers to self-identity, to identity to the same. It designates a reality which is if possible fixed, not subject to change, not modifiable by the event nor by the other. In this way it has something in common with the Platonic idea.

Relational identity goes counter to this solipsistic, neuter, auto-logical ideal. It contests the cleavages sensible/intelligible, concrete/abstract, matter/form, living/dead. It also refuses the opposition between being and becoming, and the fact that the plural of the *one* would be the multiple before being the *two*. Relational identity considers the concrete identity which is always identity in relation. As such, it is always metastable, becoming. What I try to think is the articulation between the constant transformation required by a living connection to nature and a return to self which permits a being – and a remaining – self in the process of becoming. I find this place of articulation in the belonging to a gender and in the faithfulness to the fulfilment of this gender. The fact of being a woman, and of having to always realize my own gender more perfectly, provides me with an anchoring in an identity which must not for all that be fixed and unchanged. The specificity of this identity is furthermore linked to a particular relational universe. The girl's relation to she who engendered her is other than that of the boy: the girl is born of one who is the same as her, she can beget like her mother, which is not the case for the boy.

Woman's corporeal identity is also accompanied by relational characters different than those of man: to make love and to engender inside oneself do not put one into relation with the other in the same way as making love and engendering outside the self.

When I speak of relational identity, I designate that economy of relations to the self, to the world and to the other specific to woman or to man. This identity is structured between natural given and cultural construction. Cultivating one's natural identity would signify becoming more and more able to elaborate a universe of relations both faithful to the self and capable of communication with the other, in particular with the different other, belonging to a gender other than mine.

S.P. and H.B.: What is the status of the intersubjective relation proposed in *I Love to You*? Do women establish such a relation more easily than men? Is this a type of relation that you often experience in your own life?

L.I.: In *I Love to You*, I try to define the possibility of the intersubjective relationship itself. In the Western tradition, this question is almost absent. But it represents an important dimension in the constitution of the subject. The masculine subject less attends to this than the feminine subject. This probably explains why it was the task of a woman to begin treating philosophically the relation between subjects.

The fact that I approached the problem beginning with the political level is not an accident. It is on this level that masculine philosophers have at times spoken of the relations between individuals. But it was a question then of relations between individuals defined in the socio-cultural organization of the world of between-men: the city, the nation, even the religious group. It was never a question – except in an abstract manner? – of the relation between two individuals here and now present one to the other, even, in fact, in the context of marriage. Speaking of the intersubjective relation in connection with a political encounter allowed me to reveal the difference between a feminine conception and a masculine conception of the civil relation. Personally, I consider that the civil relation must be founded upon a real rapport between two concrete individuals. I do not therefore submit the citizens to models, represented by ideas or authorities, but I invite them to a conviviality which permits the construction of a peaceful and harmonious community. Let us say that I start off from the base and not from the summit, as our tradition generally does. It is interesting to note that, furthermore, this brings me to approach as a priority the question of coexistence in the respect for differences, whereas a society elaborated according to an 'idea' is elaborated with the hypothesis of equal citizens.

Moreover, I wrote *I Love to You* because of necessities which presented themselves to me: how to engage in politics with a man in respecting our differences, of gender first of all, then of culture, of language, of education, and so on. *I Love to You* corresponds to a small treatise on political philosophy that aims towards a democratic organization of civil community. It is amusing to find that while theorists of the same problem claim to found the community on money, on goods, on the army, and so on. I start from love between a man and a woman capable of surmounting instinct, or immediate attraction, in order to cement, by their desire, a living civil community. I think that this gesture is indispensable today, including against the death drives which risk disintegrating any society.

S.P. and H.B.: Given that the relational identity of a woman is very different than that of a man, how can these differences be negotiated in order to create a satisfying intersubjectivity between women and men? Is it necessary, for example, for men to modify their relational identity?

L.I.: Men *and* women must modify their relational identity. Certainly, women 'spontaneously' privilege the relation between subjects and men the relation to objects. The feminine subject constructs itself through a relation to the other, the masculine subject through the manufacture of objects and worlds starting from which it is possible for him to exchange with the other. Let us say that woman must learn to put some objectivity susceptible to being shared between *I* and *you*: this relation must not remain, for her, at the level of need and of subjective immediacy, otherwise the *you* risks disappearing as *you*. The man, on the other hand, needs to rediscover the other as subject beyond his universe of objects. What the one and the other lack in order to realize their relation is a dialectic between subjectivity and objectivity, at the same time proper to each and common.

The dimension of *gender* can supply the existence of such a dialectic. Belonging to a gender implies determinations at the same time subjective and objective. In respecting them, in and for themselves and between them, the feminine subject and the masculine subject can communicate beyond their belonging to a specific relational identity: the woman renouncing a sensible, affective immediacy, in the relation to the other, and man renouncing a privileging of the object which often leads him to consider the other as object. In such a perspective, there no longer exists a subject in some way neuter and interchangeable. Each subject is indexed under a gender and addresses another subject which is equally so: I*she* addresses you*he*, for example. This calls for the construction of new types of mediations allowing an inter-communication between the genders which is not reducible to need, nor to instinct, nor to natural fecundity, etc.

S.P. and H.B.: How can one encourage people to recognize, in their own lives, the potential for intersubjective relations like the one you describe in *I Love to You*? That is to say, how can one encourage people to rethink their way of understanding identity and relation?

L.I.: A first means or way would be perhaps to bring women and men to reflect on the rapport that exists between the extent of their attraction for one another and the extent of their disappointment in the face of the short duration of this attraction. It would be possible then to understand that this widespread reality results from a non-respected difference of identity. This realization can take place, in a mixed group, through the composition of sentences integrating one or more words of relational significance – 'with', 'together', 'to share', 'I . . . you', and so on. – and the comparison of sentences produced by men and by women. I have already verified, on numerous occasions, how such a simple exercise aids the self-awareness of proper identity and of the difference linked to gender. It is desirable, in the same encounter, to invite, alternately, a woman and a man to speak to a man and a woman proposing to him or her a plan to be shared, which takes into consideration the two identities. This learning is not only welcomed but even desired as much by adults as by children. I have practiced this many times, particularly in Italy working on 'Education towards citizenship in the respect for difference(s)'.

Another way is to point out that a democratic politics is impossible without respect for the identity of each person. It is important therefore to cultivate a real relation between citizens. For lack of doing this, the subjection and oppression of some by others exists, as well as the growth of an abstract energy which serves authoritarian, totalitarian regimes much more than it serves democratic politics.

S.P. and H.B.: In your phenomenology of the caress, you speak of the importance of the negative, of mystery and of the invisible between two subjects in relation. Could you comment on these concepts, on their place in your theory, and on the implications which proceed from the inclusion of such notions in a philosophical theory of relational identity?

L.I.: The caress seems to me an exemplary gesture at the crossroads of civil exchange and private exchange. It marks the passage of the relation from a link of citizenship to a more carnal, more intimate link: the link between lovers, the one also between parents and children, natural or otherwise. It is about the caress between lovers that I have tried to outline a phenomenology. In part in order to distinguish what I have said about the caress in the perspective of a philosophy of two sexually different subjects from what philosophers such as Sartre, Merleau-Ponty, Levinas have said about it. For these philosophers, the caress is not a reciprocal gesture capable of bringing about an awakening to another level of intersubjectivity; it is a gesture of seduction, of capture, of appropriation practiced by lovers not identified sexually (neuter?) one towards the other, or by man towards woman. In order to go out of this absence of humanity in the carnal rapport, it is necessary to make sexual difference pass from the level of simple naturalness, of instinct, to that of a sexuated subjectivity, respectful of the self and the other. This implies a recognition of the other as the representative of a part of nature and spirituality irreducible to the part that I represent. Encountering the other, I must affirm and repeat: *you, who will never be I, nor me, nor mine*. Which supposes, on my part, the consciousness and acceptance that I cannot be the whole of nature nor of spirit: *I will never be you, nor yours*. My subjectivity is constituted in the relation to the other starting from a *not*, from a negativity unassumable (without possible *Aufhebung*) into an absolute, whatever it may be. No one absolute can abolish the difference between the man-subject and the woman-subject. Sexual difference compels us to a radical refounding of dialectic, of ontology, of theology. The negative, the mystery of the unknowable, are unsurpassable in the sexuated relation, without abolishing one of the subjects and blinding oneself by such a gesture. Each represents for the other a beyond of the visible, of the perceptible, by the senses and consciousness, which is a source of desire and of humanity and which can in no way be reduced.

These dimensions of the negative, of the mystery, of the invisible are fundamental in the philosophy of subjectivity that I try to construct. They represent a questioning of the foundations of what we call intelligible, *epistémé*, reason, idea, concept, etc. But they signify one more step in the becoming of human consciousness, liberty, ethics, a stage where ethics is not separated from ontology but remains linked to it as access to the world of another light where the 'mystery of the other illuminates' on the path of a new rationality.

S.P. and H.B.: In *I Love to You* you write:

> Without doubt, the most appropriate content for the universal is sexual difference. Indeed, this content is both real and universal. Sexual difference is an immediate natural given and it is a real and irreducible component of the universal. The whole of human kind is composed of women and men and of nothing else. The problem of race is, in fact, a secondary problem – except from a geographical point of view? – which means we cannot see the wood for the trees, and the same goes for other cultural diversities – religious, economic and political ones.
>
> Sexual difference probably represents the most universal question we can address. Our era is faced with the task of dealing with this issue, because, across the whole world, there are, there are only, men and women. (*I Love to You*, p. 47)

In what sense is sexual difference the most appropriate content for the universal? How do you respond to those who see in this privileging of sexual difference a luxury due to class, racial or cultural privilege? That is to say, even though sexual difference is or seems to be the most appropriate content for the universal from the point of view of a white bourgeois European intellectual woman, is it possible that this privileging of sexual difference is nothing but a privileging of the most classic sort?

L.I.: Sexual difference is a given of reality. It belongs universally to all humans. Being interested in it cannot, in any case, result from any privilege, but forgetting its importance can. Because the way in which sexual relations are organized in a society, in a culture, can create privileges. It is therefore decisive, for a democratic management of the community, to define relations between the genders which avoid all hierarchy. This requires a rearticulation of the passages between nature and culture while considering the concrete reality of man and woman and the manner in which this concrete reality can be structured at the symbolic level. Rules of exchange must then be established which allow communication between the worlds specific to each gender, while recognizing an equivalent value in each one of these worlds.

This change of social organization can permit us to approach the problems of multiculturalism and globalization which appear as a given of history to resolve. In the entire world, there exists only men and women. To succeed in treating democratically this universal reality is a way to accomplish the task that the development of civilizations constrains us to carry out. It is interesting to note, related to this, that certain differences between cultures come from more or less hierarchical treatments of the relations between the genders, at the horizontal or genealogical level. Abolishing the rights and privileges of one gender over another signifies therefore working for the possibility of a world culture. But this can happen only in the respect for differences, in order to avoid this culture being abstract and not real.

Translation from the French by Stephen Pluháček, Heidi Bostic and Luce Irigaray.

Bibliography

The questions of Stephen Pluháček and Heidi Bostic are formulated starting from the following texts:

Luce Irigaray, *Speculum. De l'autre femme* (Paris: Minuit, 1974); trans. Gillian C. Gill as *Speculum: Of the Other Woman* (Ithaca, NY: Cornell University Press, 1985).

—— *Ce sexe qui n'en est pas un* (Paris: Minuit, 1977); trans. Catherine Porter with Carolyn Burke as *This Sex Which is Not One* (Ithaca, NY: Cornell University Press, 1985), especially 'The Mechanics of Fluids'.

—— *Amante marine. De Friedrich Nietzsche* (Paris: Minuit, 1980); trans. Gillian C. Gill as *Marine Lover: Of Friedrich Nietzsche* (New York: Columbia University Press, 1991).

—— *Passions élémentaires* (Paris: Minuit, 1982); trans. Joanne Collie and Judith Still as *Elemental Passions* (London and New York: Continuum and Routledge, 1992).

—— *L'oubli de l'air. Chez Martin Heidegger* (Paris: Minuit, 1983); trans. Mary Beth Mader as *The Forgetting of Air: In Martin Heidegger* (Austin and London: University of Texas Press and Continuum, 1999).

—— *Éthique de la différence sexuelle* (Paris: Minuit, 1984); trans. Carolyn Burke and Gillian C. Gill as *An Ethics of Sexual Difference* (Ithaca, New York and London: Cornell University Press and Continuum, 1993).

—— *Parler n'est jamais neutre* (Paris: Minuit, 1985), especially 'Le sujet de la science est-il sexué?' trans. Gail Schwab, as *To Speak Is Never Neutral* (New York and London: Continuum, 2000).

—— *Sexes et parentés* (Paris: Minuit, 1987); trans. Gillian C. Gill as *Sexes and Genealogies* (New York: Columbia University Press, 1993).

—— *Le sexe linguistique* (*Langages* 85; ed. Luce Irigaray; Paris: Larousse, 1987).

—— *Le Temps de la différence: Pour une révolution pacifique* (Paris: Librairie générale française [livre de poche], 1989); trans. Karin Montin as *Thinking the Difference: For a Peaceful Revolution* (London and New York: Continuum and Routledge, 1994).

—— *Je, tu, nous: Pour une culture de la différence* (Paris: Grasset, 1990); trans. Alison Martin as *Je, tu, nous: Towards a Culture of Difference* (London and New York: Routledge, 1993).

—— *Sexes et genres à travers les langues* (Paris: Grasset, 1990).

—— *J'aime à toi: Esquisse d'une félicité dans l'Histoire* (Paris: Grasset, 1992); trans. Alison Martin as *I Love to You: Sketch for a Felicity Within History* (London and New York: Routledge, 1996).

—— *Genres culturels et interculturels* (*Langages* 111; ed. Luce Irigaray; Paris: Larousse, 1993), especially 'Importance du genre dans la constitution de la subjectivité et de l'intersubjectivité'.

—— 'Femmes et hommes , une identité relationnelle différente', in *La place des femmes. Les enjeux de l'identité et de l'égalité au regard des sciences sociales* (ed. Ephesia; Paris: La Découverte, 1995).

'Towards a Wisdom of Love'

Conversation between

Luce Irigaray and Judith Still

Judith Still: This dialogue is a special occasion in that it follows the launch of two new publications: a collection edited by Luce Irigaray entitled *Dialogues* and a new monograph *The Way of Love*. *Dialogues* is the proceedings of a conference hosted by Griselda Pollock in Leeds – at the AHRB Centre for Cultural Analysis, Theory and History – in June 2001, in which a paper given by Luce Irigaray at the University of Nottingham also takes place ('Why Cultivate Difference?'). In this work Luce Irigaray brings together a number of scholars, including many younger academics who have recently completed, or are in the process of doing, PhDs on her work. They came from, amongst other places: the UK of course, but also Holland, Italy, Finland, North America, Canada and Mexico. The intention was to make the dialogue intercultural, international and intergenerational. The journal *Paragraph*, brought out by Edinburgh University Press, offered to publish the proceedings in a volume unique amongst Luce Irigaray's work in that it does not only include two of her own articles, her Introduction and her Conclusion, but also her questions to the participants and their responses. *The Way of Love* is a beautiful book which shows us Luce Irigaray as philosopher-poet – in other books she may be a researcher in socio-linguistics, a therapist, a teacher or someone who speaks very clearly and directly to non-specialists of the need for political change. She is a philosopher in a different etymological sense to the one usually privileged by our society and certainly by the Academy. She is not the dry, would-be universal master of philosophy who instructs us to love 'wisdom' – his wisdom. She wishes as a poet, a creator, as well as a philosopher, to suggest to us that not only do we need to attend to the mind but also to our bodies, and not only to the same ones, but also to the other(s), those who are different from ourselves. She suggests philosophy as *the wisdom of love.*

The format of this conversation is a mixture of Luce Irigaray's responses to my questions and my reading extracts from her new work.

* * *

JUDITH STILL:

> The wisdom of love is perhaps the first meaning of the word 'philosophy' . . .
>
> Confused with a conceptual translation of the real, a formal knowledge, *sophia* is often reduced to a mental exercise, passed on from a master to disciples, of use in populating universities and in having discussions among the initiated but without the impact on our lives that a wisdom presupposes. The presumed friend of wisdom becomes, from then on, one who falls into wells due to an inability to walk up on the earth. His science causes laughter like that of other sages just as incapable of governing their life and who nevertheless issue words claiming to instruct us on the most everyday and the most sublime. Between the head and the feet, a continuity is lost, a perspective has not been constructed. And the wisdom of which these technicians of the logos are enamoured is sometimes a knowing how to die, but seldom the apprenticeship to a knowing how to live. (*The Way of Love*, pp. 1–3)

Could you tell us some more about this 'wisdom of love'?

LUCE IRIGARAY: Philosophy has been understood in our Western tradition as: love of wisdom. Now, it was possible to hear this word as: wisdom of love as well, as it is the case for 'theosophy' understood as: wisdom of God, for example. But it is true that 'theosophy' is endowed with rather negative connotations in comparison with 'theology'. What thus has occurred between *sophia* and *logos*, that is, between wisdom and Western logic? At the beginning of our culture, it is the Goddess who unveils the truth to the philosopher, as we read in the texts of some Pre-Socratics, for example Parmenides and Empedocles. But the male philosopher lacks the means for expressing such a revelation. And, even if he has been illuminated by it, the master does not pass on the teaching of the Goddess. This will remain a 'Source', a 'Being', a 'Thing', and even a 'Hole' which stays beyond his wisdom, a positive Absolute that has been experienced by some Pre-Socratics. But, as they could not express and impart this experience, they progressively forgot it and transformed it, at best, into emptiness. The Pre-Socratic philosophers, in fact, begin to substitute the love of wisdom for the wisdom of love. With this gesture, they exclude the words of and about her – Goddess, woman, nature – from the Western wisdom and its transmission. This transmission, from then on, takes place between a male master and a spiritual son. And the condition of such a teaching requires logical rules which cut the discourse off from a sensible experience and, above all, from relations with a world and a wisdom in the feminine.

The Pre-Socratic master will increasingly lack means for passing on, and even remembering, the meeting with her – Goddess, woman, nature. All these means are somehow related to language itself. Now the choice of 'the love of wisdom' rather than 'the wisdom of love' appears as a choice of men, who prefer (as I could observe through an important experimental work) the relation between subject and object – love of wisdom as an object – to the relation between subjects – that the wisdom of love involves.

J.S.: Could we discuss your own relation to, and interest in, *language*? Your first language is French. Why have you chosen to write sometimes in Italian, sometimes in English as in *Dialogues*? Translation is an important issue in *Dialogues*, and one which you highlight in your preface to *The Way of Love*. Could you also say something about the problems of translation?

L.I.: We know that the girls take a particular interest in language. It was, it is, the case for me. I am not especially interested in language already constituted, in *logos*, except as a way of understanding my tradition and masculine subjectivity. It also represents an occasion for playing with words, with argumentation and so on. My principal interest in language does not consist in repeating already coded meanings but in creating new meanings in order to speak in the present: to enter into relation with the world, the other(s) and also myself in the present. Speaking-with, for me as a woman, is preferred to speaking-of, and communicating-with to communicating information. Poetry itself is experienced by me as a means of entering in relation in a more global way, of being more totally with the other.

Perhaps this explains my wish to translate myself my texts in other languages. A translator cannot, and furthermore may not, have, with respect to a text, the same creativity, nor the same liberty, as the writer herself. When my texts are translated by someone other, often I find that my thinking or speaking has become a little dead. They are separated from the body, the soul, the breath and the heart which engendered them. Thus, I have learned at least Italian and English, the languages of the two countries or cultures with whom I most work. This also bears witness to my desire to communicate with the readers whom I meet through my books. Translating is too a relation with language which seems to me an important task, above all when alternating with a work of philosophy strictly speaking. This task is useful both for keeping a scientific rigour and for relaxing. As is the case with the analysis of language or discourse that I practice.

J.S.: You have directed research in numerous countries on the language of children; this work is less well known in England than some of your other writings – could you tell us a little about it?

L.I.: I have worked a lot on the analysis of language or discourse – poetic language in a first time, later pathological language, and now above all sexuate language and discourse. I wanted to make apparent what could signify the difference between men and women beyond their biological or sociological belonging. I wanted also to discover if the difference between the sexes represents a universal which crosses the boundaries of languages and cultures, and to verify if women's way of speaking bears witness to an alienation or to another world with respect to men's discourse. The analysis of language produced by boys and girls is crucial for this question. This part of my research on the sexuation of discourse and communication between the sexes is anyway particularly important. The relational life of little children is not yet concealed or distorted by educational programmes and they have fewer ideological resistances towards the sexually different.

What types of utterances are produced by children approximately eight years old to the cue asking to make a sentence with the words 'with', 'together', 'to love', 'to share', for example? The girls produce sentences as 'I talk with Marco', 'Marco and I have a child together', 'I am madly in love with Gian Paolo', 'I share with Dylan even though I never really met with him'. The boys, for their part, make sentences as: 'I hit the ball with the racket', 'I always play together with them' (other boys, according to the context of their discourse), 'I love basketball', 'I share the computer with my mom'. One can thus notice that the girls prefer relations between subjects, relations in difference and between two persons, horizontal relations, while the boys prefer relations between subject and object, relations with the same as them in the one–many configuration, and hierarchical or family relations. Does this difference signify an alienation of girls dating from birth, if not before? Research carried out on significant populations of girls and boys indicates the contrary. Girls show themselves to be more precocious in literary terms, artistically and linguistically than boys. They are more creative as well. Which results from their more developed relational life. Unfortunately, education – as our whole culture, including philosophy – is still based on the characteristics of the male subjectivity, and is seldom concerned with the values peculiar to the female subjectivity. And what is especially lacking is a cultivation of horizontal relations between different subjects. One could say: a wisdom of love.

J.S.: Your relation to philosophers, as well as to philosophy, is an interesting one. Philosophers are sometimes described in your work as playing games, talking to those who are like themselves, whether talking to equals or as masters to disciples; which means a sort of monologue that produces a *partial* truth. You ask them to talk to, and listen to, those who are different, to women in particular – and thus to inaugurate a dialogue. Usually philosophers choose to speak *about* objects instead of speaking *with* other subjects, particularly subjects different from them as women are. Is Heidegger a masculine philosopher who speaks as a subject about objects? How would you describe your relation to Heidegger – one of the four voices in *The Way of Love*? Even though he cannot reply exactly, can it be termed a dialogue or amorous exchange?

L.I.: Heidegger is a philosopher whom I read and read again. My copies of his texts have notes of different years where I read them. Heidegger constrains you to think with rigour. He is also the philosopher who practices the most criticism towards himself. Sometimes, reading the text of Heidegger, I write 'no' in the margin, or '??', or '!!' He is the only philosopher who, a few pages later, answers my critiques or questions. Never can I make fun of his argumentation as is the case for many other philosophers. I solely smile thinking: that is truly a masculine way of reasoning. Nevertheless, Heidegger does not remain simply in a subject–object problematic. In his work, 'thing' sometimes takes the place of 'object', and 'thing' represents a more complex reality in which he invests a part of what could intervene in the relations with another person. But Heidegger seldom enters into a dialogue with another subject, above all a subject of another sex. He stops at dialogue with another culture, another language. In this case, the exchange is about something, not between two subjects. The accent is still put on the objectivity of the thing to be considered not on intersubjectivity as such.

Generally Heidegger converses with himself through language. Language is the principal 'thing' he considers. And, as a 'thing', language speaks to him. He remains conversing with language in his linguistic house, without asking himself if someone could really speak another language than his. He stays in his own linguistic dwelling hoping that some deity could bring there something unexpected. Heidegger has probably made the most radical criticism of Western philosophy and culture. But, to leave his house of language, perhaps he needed a woman – to allude to Nietzsche's assertion that: to go further, a woman is necessary for me.

Could I confess that I deeply regret that I did not have the opportunity to converse with Heidegger? Certainly I do that through his texts, but I would prefer to converse with the man himself. Perhaps I am mistaken here, but it is the case. And when I learnt about the death of the philosopher, it was difficult for me to accept that I will never talk with him.

Of course I know the reproaches addressed to Heidegger. He also addressed them to himself. I hope that people who stop at reproaches towards him do not intend, in this way, to escape thinking. And I am sure that they also have reproaches to address to themselves, as is the case for all of us. Perhaps they do not know in what they have failed and they are still failing.

J.S.:

> Air is what is left common between subjects living in different worlds. It is the elemental of the universe, of the life starting from which it is possible to elaborate the transcendental. Air is that in which we dwell and which dwells in us, in varied ways without doubt, but providing for passages between – in ourselves, between us. Air is the medium of our natural and spiritual life, of our relation to ourselves, to speaking, to the other. And this medium imperceptibly crosses the limits of different worlds or universes, sometimes giving the illusion of a gained intimacy

while we are only sharing a common element. (*The Way of Love*, pp. 67–68)

You have already written a book on Heidegger and the element of air. The importance of air returns here, for instance, air as virgin space, common between us, in which we dwell and which dwells in us. Could you tell us – particularly non-specialists – a little more about this?

L.I.: I could add that I am surprised that Heidegger did not care more about air, sometimes asserting that considering this dimension belongs only to the domain of science. Perhaps it is the way of acceding to intersubjectivity which was lacking to him. Recognizing air as a medium is necessary to reach a relationship with the other, the other as different, and in particular as sexually different. I explained, in *The Forgetting of Air*, how the oblivion of air results from the non-elaboration of the originary link with the mother. Before our birth, our mother provided us with oxygen through her blood. We scarcely remember this first gift of life, sometimes transferring it onto God himself, without paying our debt to our mother, not even in thought. After our being born, air is that which gives us first autonomy as living beings. We also forget that most of the time, and thus we lose our autonomy. Now, in order to be two, to meet with the other with respect for our respective differences, and to welcome and love the other as other, autonomy is necessary. If we do not care about our autonomy, we generally return to a fusional relation, to an undifferentiated world or to a group formed by somebodies. All these situations prevent us from entering into presence with the other, and also entails a risk of autoritarianism and totalitarianism. Sharing air is not sufficient to maintain the two, but cultivating one's own breathing is needed to keep one's own autonomy and the difference between us, especially as two. I could add, on this subject, that pollution does not damage only our health but our relational life, depriving us of the air that is necessary for securing our autonomy.

J.S.: You refer to autonomy, to being two – I wonder if we could move on to one relation between two that has been of particular interest to me in my own work on *Feminine Economies*. You write on a number of occasions about giving, and you specify here that it is not so much a gift of things as of words. This suggests a different kind of economy to the one in which we live a great part of our lives, i.e., the market in which everything must be quantified, a market economy in which everything is 'valued', but in which we cannot value true value. Could you say some more about the gift, sharing, or exchange of language?

L.I.: I take interest above all in how we could share what is not representable nor possible to evaluate: what occurs between mother and foetus before birth, or between lovers, for example. How can we practice reciprocity there? This kind of sharing is today recovered by an economy of market in which everything is quantified and payable, according to a price more or less arbitrary. The solution of the gift that you propose in your *Feminine Economies* is certainly useful to cut into the uniformity of an economy of market. I wonder whether it is sufficient to reach a reciprocity between two, unless the gift be not only a gift of something but also a gift of life, of breath, of love. Perhaps to succeed in doing that sharing language could be more of help than giving things. Of course it is not a question here of communicating only information between us but of joining another way of speaking – speaking-with more than speaking-of – as I try to do in *The Way of Love*, and already in *I Love to You* or *To Be Two*. Doing that, sharing language is then understood as sharing language strictly speaking but also as sharing gestures, and more generally as sharing space and time. We have to invent and to practice a new culture, a culture in which relations between subjects prevail over relations of a subject with objects, or even through objects, as is generally the case in our masculine Western culture.

A few words more: as I have already said, a thing does not simply amount to an object, and all things are not endowed with the same meaning as regard to intersubjectivity. Sometimes we can find things which bear witness to this unrepresentable and invaluable sharing of breath, of heart or love to which I alluded. But an access to another way of speaking to each other will help us in discovering, and above all in creating, such things.

J.S.:

> The other cannot be kept, sheltered thanks to a simple decision. Irreducible to us, we cannot apprehend the other in order to provide a dwelling for them. This place of hospitality for the other becomes built as much as, if not more than, we build it deliberately. Made of our flesh, of our heart, and not only of words, it demands that we accept that it takes place without our unilaterally overseeing its construction. It is in

> secret that it unfolds without any mastery by our seeing, by our domination through language. Remaining hidden, the other can be safeguarded. And it is certainly not when unveiling that we can protect what the other is as other nor prepare the path going to meet with them.
>
> Our tradition, founded upon the intelligibility, the mastery, the unveiling for us of that which is, has prevented the approach to the other through gestures and words that disturb the entering into presence with him, or her. (*The Way of Love*, pp. 154–55)

Another term which comes to my mind is 'hospitality', a question much debated in French philosophy at the moment, and a question which relates both to the most intimate domains, and to the political with the issue of refugees, for example. What would you say on the subject of hospitality?

L.I.: In my opinion, hospitality needs a culture of difference and a culture of desire. Perhaps the two correspond to one only requirement: being able to welcome the other as other. Generally we admit the other amongst us on the condition that the other takes up our culture, our habits, our beliefs, our language. We agree with laying out a space in our country, our home, our mind for the other who has in some away become like us. We go along with generosity, paternalistic condescension but not with modification of our way of thinking and acting, especially without any leaving the logic of sameness which rules Western culture for centuries. We thus ask the other to become the same as ourselves, unless we give ourselves up to become the same as the other. Now a culture which claims to be global, to respect the other as child, woman or foreigner must have access to another logic, a logic taking difference into account – not a quantitative difference which in fact remains in sameness, but a qualitative irreducible difference between subjects who cannot substitute the one for the other nor share the same world. This presupposes entering in a culture of desire, and not only a culture of needs. Sharing needs can accompany a logic of sameness. But does such a sharing reach a human culture? Could giving to the other only shelter, food, money, signify giving hospitality? Certainly it is better than leaving the other dying of cold or hunger. But stopping at this level is not yet offering hospitality. Sometimes it is a question of morality, a morality which seeks to satisfy its own consciousness, but it is not yet to share with another through hospitality – a gesture that requires sharing oneself, that is sharing at the level of being and not only of having.

J.S.:

> From the other irradiates a truth which we can receive without its source being visible. That from which the other elaborates a meaning remains a mystery for us, but we can indirectly perceive something of it. Such an operation transforms the subject, enlightens the subject in a way that is both visible and invisible. The light that then reaches us illuminates the world otherwise, and discloses to us the particularity of our point of view. It says nothing in a way, pronounces no word but makes clear the limits of a horizon, of a site of thinking, of existing, of Being. (*The Way of Love*, p. 164)

A word you often use is *becoming* – for example, human becoming. And you say that a word whose meaning is not already completely known could allow becoming, because we can be touched by words and moved by them (in both senses). But what does this term becoming mean to you?

L.I.: I alternately say: 'human becoming' and 'becoming human'. The step in our human becoming about which I speak could, in fact and finally, be a becoming human. I do not consider that we fulfill our humanity from birth. Certainly we have a genetic human inheritance but it only signifies to have the potential to reach our humanity. This capability has too often been valued in a quantitative way in relation to other species or kingdoms: being human would amount to having a greater number of nervous cells, which allows us to perform more and better. I do not think that our humanity can be reduced to that. And I consider that we are mistaken when we interpret our difference in relation to other species or kingdoms as a quantitative difference. In fact, we then remain belonging to the species or kingdoms from which we claim to differ.

It seems to me that it is more through relational behaviour that we can accomplish our humanity. Sexuate difference takes on a crucial interest here. It corresponds to the level where we reach, or not, a being human. Transforming our instincts and drives in a sharing of love, of words, of thought is a way of becoming humans. The question is not whether we are capable of renouncing sexual attraction but whether we can transmute it into human sharing between us. That requires us to have access to another stage of our becoming. We have considered this becoming as a solitary journey from a natural state to a cultural or spiritual state. But that end somehow means leaving our humanity in order to join an ideal or an absolute: Truth or God, for example. Thus, we do not fulfil our humanity as such, we give it up for Truth or God. A human becoming rather implies to accomplish our being human, especially through our way of being in relation with the other. Becoming, then, no longer corresponds to a solitary journey: it is, at each step, determined by the relations to and with the other. Not only the other who shares the same ideal or Absolute as me, and with whom I can move towards them, but also the other who belongs to another world, and whom I must take into account as a human different from myself. I always meet this other at a crossroads between two becomings, and I have to be faithful to my becoming and also to the becoming of the other, whom I must let be without confusing him or her with a part of myself. This dimension of our human becoming has not sufficiently been considered in Western tradition. Caring about sexuate difference between us can help us to open up to a new stage of becoming human(s). Sexuate difference provides us with limits which allow both opening up to the other and returning to the self – two gestures necessary in the process of becoming human.

J.S.: You suggest that we need to re-think the relation with the *mother*. It is the relation with the mother that is the engendering ground and one that allows both body and mind to remain present. The law of the father might be said to cut us off from the relation with the other as living being. What we need is a different introduction to negativity – one that would safeguard difference instead of abolishing it. Is it right to say that this *thinking* of the relation with the mother might help create a third place in common, a world to be shared?

L.I.: Being conscious of, and cultivating one's own relation with the mother is crucial to reach sharing in difference. It is a necessary condition on the part of man to escape a lack of differentiation from his natural origin without succeeding in this only through a repression of his relational life by substituting objects – material or spiritual – for another subject, or by projecting the first other, the maternal other, onto a God of his own gender; which prevents man from entering into relation with a different other, especially a sexually different other. A woman has to make another path. If the relation with another subject is easier for her because she has the same gender as her mother, she has to gain her autonomy with respect to a mother to whom she is similar, at the level of being, of possible having and as regards to origin. She has to construct a relation with the other which escapes a natural and empirical status. It is through the respect of the other as transcending her that she can differ from identification with her mother while avoiding a rejection of her. The other who is horizontally transcending woman is the other of a different gender: be they a lover, a friend and even a son. Through respecting this other as irreducible to her apprehension, whether sensible or mental, woman can emerge from a natural status that comes into her subjectivity, and reach a cultural identity.

Thus both man and woman, each in their own way, have to solve their original relation with the mother in order to open a space for meeting together. But the relationship with the mother cannot constitute a common third place in which to share together. It is through a specific cultivation of this relationship from the part of the boy and the girl, of man and woman, that the space for an encounter in difference can be opened. We thus are far from the third term that the law of the father would represent through the imposition of a common language, culture, religion to be shared by both men and women.

J.S.:

> To hold a dialogue is another thing. And it is manifest that, for most of us, we have hardly attained such a kind of exchange . . . But, at least, we have tried, and we have begun to understand the difficulty of holding a dialogue, also and perhaps above all between subjects of the same gender. I hope that we will go further on this path, each for their own part and also together. And thus discover little by little what it could signify to communicate between us taking into account our respective differences. Then we will search for words, for syntax, for gestures – also talking gestures such as keeping silent, listening to, praising, offering beauty through speech, and so on. – capable of giving and receiving meaning, not only about things or an already existing world, but about ourselves, and one another – with our bodies, desires, hearts, souls, thoughts, ideals. (*Dialogues*, p. 209)

This extract returns us to the question of how, granted our differences, we can and should speak to each other.

L.I.: If we remain enclosed within the horizon of an uncultured relation with the mother, we cannot really speak to each other. Of course, we can exchange at the level of needs, of information, but we cannot hold a dialogue. We are then separated by a different relation to origin, a difference of which we are neither conscious nor capable to escape. We converse through a supposed third dimension imposed on us: a same language, a same world, but those are constructed more or less artificially towards nature and towards ourselves. Furthermore, they are constructed only by one of us not by the two. Thus, we cannot really share such a third, unless we distance ourselves from ourselves and do not exchange as people who are different and respect their difference(s). Such difference(s) presuppose that we listen to one another, not only to a discourse already coded but to a subjectivity irreducible to ours. This listening must always be a precondition to not sacrifice the other to a virtual object of our discourse nor subject ourselves to a discourse which is not our own. Language itself must take into consideration the present dialogue without stopping at an exchange of pieces of information already defined outside the meeting between the two. Entering into dialogue requires us to use a language which touches, which involves sensibility, which preserves the role of the other in the constitution of meaning. We have to invent, to create a new way of talking together, in which not only the mind is concerned but all that we are. Art then recovers a place that Western logic has too neglected in our exchanges, as it is also the case with concern about the present. A dialogue is always a creation which takes place in a meeting between two persons; it cannot be reduced to a repetition of something already said in another time, another context.

J.S.:

> The rift between the other and me is irreducible. To be sure we can build bridges, join our energies, feast and celebrate encounters, but the union is never definitive, on pain of no longer existing. Union implies returning into oneself, moving away, dissenting, separating. To correspond with one's own becoming requires an alternation of approaching the other and dividing from him, or her. (*The Way of Love*, p. 157)

Can we talk about the relation between dialogue and love? There are many different ways of thinking about, or experiencing, love. It can be seen as an occasion for production – making children for instance. It can be seen to derive from the need to satisfy our instincts. It may be a kind of appropriation. Plato's *Symposium* puts forward, amongst others, the notion that we need to find our 'other halves' – an idea of reunification, of complementing an amputated being that you challenge. Am I right to think that you want to suggest a path towards a different, more truly human, kind of love that requires three elements: a masculine subject, a feminine subject – that is, two different subjects, whose the most basic paradigm lies in sexuate difference – and a relationship which needs a third place, a virgin place *between* the two? Could you talk about the importance of love a little more?

L.I.: Without dialogue, love in difference is not possible. Most of the time, we remain, with respect to the other(s), in a sort of filial or family feeling, a feeling that can be passion but not love in difference. As for dialogue, love requires a constant care and creativity. It is no longer a question of simply feeling but of making love exist through a faithfulness to the other without relinquishing oneself. Once more, the problem is how to remain two in love, two different subjects who maintain an interval between them, which belongs neither to the one nor to the other. This intervention of the negative between the two is possible without breaking the relationship; on the contrary it keeps desire alive between them. Each can thus dwell in the limits of one's own world and also meet with the other beyond these limits. In this way, a third world becomes built, which is not imposed on the two by a supposedly common world already there, but which is constructed by the two as both the result and the possibility of love. Building such a common world, which belongs neither to the one nor to the other, is a fruit of love and a way of accomplishing this love and making it blossom. The matter now is one of loving, even making love, and engendering in difference, without remaining in a natural state. In such a process, love and desire cannot be separated and they together ensure the movement which goes towards the other and returns to the self, in the self, to experience and cultivate the effects of the encounter and prepare a future meeting. In this way, love in difference can assume a carnal dimension that does not amount to the mere satisfaction of instincts or drives, but leads to the most global and subtle encounter between two humans.

Bibliography

Irigaray, Luce, *L'oubli de l'air. Chez Martin Heidegger* (Paris: Minuit, 1983); trans. Mary Beth Mader as *The Forgetting of Air: In Martin Heidegger* (Austin and London: University of Texas Press and Continuum, 1999).

—— *J'aime à toi: Esquisse d'une félicité dans l'Histoire* (Paris: Grasset, 1992); trans. Alison Martin as *I Love to You: Sketch for a Felicity Within History* (London and New York: Routledge, 1996).

—— *Être Deux* (Paris: Grasset, 1997); trans. Monique M. Rhodes and Marco F. Cocito-Monoc from the Italian *Essere Due* (Torino: Bollati Boringhieri, 1994) as *To Be Two* (London and New York: Athlone and Routledge, 2000).

—— *The Way of Love*, trans. Heidi Bostic and Stephen Pluháček from the French *La Voie de l'amour* (not yet published) (London and New York: Continuum, 2002).

—— *Dialogues: Around Her Work*, special issue of *Paragraph* 25/3 (Edinburgh: Edinburgh University Press, November 2002).

Judith Still, *Feminine Economies: Thinking against the Market in the Enlightenment and the Late Twentieth Century* (Manchester: Manchester University Press, 1997).

'Oneness' and 'Being-Two' in the Practice and Culture of Yoga

Conversation between

Luce Irigaray and Michael Stone

Luce Irigaray: I received a letter from Michael Stone in July 2003. He wrote that he was editing a collection of interviews proposing an approach to yoga, which did not stop at merely physical culture and over-simplistic Indian philosophy. His intention was to explore the sophistication of yoga as a psychological practice, and to make it clear that yoga can be a practice of engagement with respect to the world in which we live through a cultivation of breath, body and mind, and not only a means to escape the world. He wanted to talk with me about the relations between sexed bodies, gendered culture and the breath, after reading my essay *Between East and West*. I sent him a written reply expressing my interest in participating, and I received a letter mentioning some practical details – about a future meeting in Paris, the length of the interview and the modalities of the work, the possibility for me to edit the interview before it became public, and even a possible payment. The letter included an initial list of questions and announced that I would receive a longer list of topics before our meeting in Paris. This encounter did not happen because of events in his family, and I, therefore, answered the list of questions that Michael Stone had sent me in writing. As this received no response, I asked about the work and the book. Michael Stone then explained to me that he was busy with editing the book, that he would soon send me a typed and edited version of our interview, but also that he met with problems on the part of the publishing house that had expressed interest in publishing the book. He added that he enjoyed reading my responses and hoped for further communication with me in the future. But this was the last message that I received from him, in spite of my attempts to enter into dialogue on the occasion of the edition of this volume of *Conversations*. I really hope that Michael Stone will appreciate that our interview will be finally published and presented to the readers that he aimed, as I do, to reach.

* * *

MICHAEL STONE: These are, of course, very basic thoughts in reference to the differences of the sexes, but they bring with them questions with regards to the language of yoga, which speaks little of the differences of gender and much of 'universals'. Is the mind universal? Can we say that there is a human psychology beyond gender, beyond culture? Even if one who is enlightened moves in such mystical realms of 'oneness' that lie beyond dualistic experience, if that person is to live in the world, he or she must do so within a culture. And culture, like language, like the body, like the mind, is gendered.

LUCE IRIGARAY: In the school in which I practice yoga, the teachers sometimes speak about a sexed yoga in an indirect way, for example a yoga fitting for gravidity – this state corresponding only to one dimension of feminine experience, a dimension that not all women live. Furthermore, the theoretical discourse of these teachers does not allude to this sexuate dimension. And my questions about a yoga appropriate to men or women are often received as ingenuous. Nevertheless, whilst travelling in India, I participated in a meeting with Krishnamacharia, the yogi who founded the school in which I practice. With great joy, I listened to his words as he recalled that the difference between the sexes is a very important dimension in the tradition. Probably those who actually do yoga have forgotten, as have we Westerners, the basic character of the sexual, and rather the sexuate, difference. We can see an evolution of this in the texts which talk of yoga.

But the fact that the sexes are two does not mean that the experience of each is dualistic. You, as man, have a certain experience of the totality and I, as woman, have another experience. Only if you remain outside yourself, you could say that difference between the sexes amounts to a dualistic experience. When you live an experience appropriate to you, this can be an experience of 'oneness' which is more or less achieved and corresponds to diverse levels, from the most material to the most transcendental. Of course such an experience is not universal because the subjects are two, and thus the universal is also dual.

To become enlightened does not presuppose that we renounce our concrete experience. And the texts linked to the practice of yoga are – at least, they were in the tradition – very connected with corporeal experience (cf., for example, *The Upanishad of the Yoga* and most of *The Yoga Sutras of Patañjali*). Breathing and energetic experience can awaken diverse chakras, becoming more and more subtle, but not for all that abstract. The mystic experience is then en-stasis rather than ek-stasis, this latter leaving the corporeal site of the self. The most important problem is how to reach enlightened en-stasis as and in two. Even if certain traditions of Hinduism present divinities as a couple, they do not comment very much about the relation between the two in the texts that I have read. Of course our Western commentators talk of two parts in a male divinity. But the sexuate characters of the divinities either at a vertical or genealogical level, or at a horizontal or amorous level are very clearly shown in the mythological stories. These characters are often associated with cosmic dimensions as I mention in the text 'The Time of Life' in *Between East and West*. They also reveal a progress in the individuation of humanity with respect to other living realms or kingdoms. Some accounts allude to the fact that the relation between masculine and feminine divinities can generate cosmic harmony or disharmony according to whether this relation is harmonious or disharmonious.

M.S.: Many students of yoga tend to move towards a worldview and corresponding language of 'oneness', which has the effect of treating others as 'essentially the same as me'. Could you talk about the dangers of using this kind of language?

L.I.: It seems to me that such behaviour does not correspond to a real experience of yoga, which is always linked to a single body. This conception of yoga seems an abstract discourse in some way separated from the body of the one who is practicing. In my opinion, the breath is never strange to the one who practices: it is more or less subtle but neither abstract nor neuter, and even the question of reaching the other could be connected with a degree of subtlety of the breath. If we remain attentive to the incarnate aspect of the practice of yoga, then we also remain attentive to the difference(s) of the other. If it is not the case, our breathing and energetic practice run the risk of being artificial and mechanical, and thus dangerous for ourselves and for others.

M.S.: To begin with, I'd like you to define some terms that you regularly use, in order to get clear on the terminology that we are sharing. What do you associate with the term 'transcendent' which you use often and in different contexts? Also, can you speak a little bit about the terms 'subjective' and 'objective' as they relate to your writings? For students of yoga, and Indian philosophy in particular, one of the first lessons is thinking through dualistic presuppositions in an effort to realize the trouble with claiming 'objective knowledge'. For Patañjali, as an example, meditation brings about an experience of the dissolution of categories such as 'subject' and 'object'. However, this tends to encourage many practitioners to think about 'sameness' or 'oneness' rather than difference. It is my personal experience, and your writings explore this, that when our preconceptions begin to drop away, we are better able to experience both oneness and difference. Your poetry at the beginning and end of *To Be Two* explores this relationship. Can you speak about the danger of leaning towards a discourse of 'sameness' and how one can integrate both the insight of oneness and the recognition of difference?

L.I.: 'Transcendent', for me, signifies that I cannot understand nor even perceive an other in its totality. I can perhaps understand or perceive some aspects but not the whole nor the origin or spring of the real I am meeting with. For example, I can understand or perceive something of the other, but not what or who the other is as such. I can perceive the other through my senses and, in part, through my mind, but the true origin and meaning of what I perceive remains hidden from me. I could say that the core of the other escapes me, and that I could not substitute myself for the other because this other remains a mystery for me. I speak here about another living being, another human being different from me – the paradigm of this difference being the sexually different other. Of course, in our tradition, transcendence generally evokes an absolutely other – God or Truth, for example. Our tradition does not take into consideration transcendence in the relations to, and with, the other, and has projected the transcendental dimension into an Absolute extraneous to our daily life, an Absolute beyond our earthly existence. This Absolute corresponds to an ideal for us, an ideal that we could not reach as we cannot reach the other in what or who he or she really are, in their difference.

It is difficult, for us Westerners, to rethink the categories of subjectivity and objectivity because they belong to the same subjective world, that of the masculine Western subject, who claims to define by himself the subjective and the objective dimensions. On my part, I rather use the term 'subjective' to talk about that which belongs to the subject as such, a subject who is not always the same, and I use 'objective' to refer to that which exists outside the subject and his, or her, intervention in a pre-given world. For example, meeting with a tree, I could say that I meet with something which is objective with respect to me. One could object that there exist ways of cultivating trees that remove them from their objective presence. One could also object that in a table made by an artisan or an artist, there remains a part of objective material while the actual form has been given by a human subjectivity. I hope that I have succeeded in explaining a little of what I try to express with 'subjective' and 'objective'.

From this perspective, overcoming the subject–object categories is not suitable. For me, 'subject' and 'object' do not correspond to constructed categories but to diverse reals. And to overcome the duality between I and another living being, in particular a human being, is not fitting, even with the aim of reaching samadhi. The question rather is how I could unite my energy with that of another living being, in particular a human being, to reach samadhi without destroying either myself or the other. With another human, above all a human of another sex, the culmination in an energetic process can be obtained through cultivating attraction while remaining in the self – which allows to live an ecstatic en-stasis. I am surprised that those who teach or simply do yoga do not care a little more about this very interesting issue regarding a culture of breath and energy in which difference could be a way to reach samadhi. Of course, it is no longer here a question of a relation between a subject and an object but between two subjects, and this presupposes an economy of energy different, including regarding the manner of gathering oneself together, concentrating, contemplating. The problem of perceiving the invisible is then more important than that of overcoming the subject–object duality.

I am afraid that remaining in sameness does not provide us with the early spring of our energy and the best cultivation of it. If we consider the culture of sameness in the West, we could observe that it is accompanied with tragedies and unhappiness. Apparently it corresponds to an easier cultivation of the self. But this is above all true for a man who needs to emerge from the maternal world by relating to and with those who are the same as himself. At least, this has been the strategy of Western man for centuries. But this solution did not bring to humanity a culture of energy and happiness nor the blossoming of the relations in difference. Furthermore, it has been associated with a domination of nature itself and not a respect for its being and growing. The woman, as mother, but not only as mother, has also suffered this exploitation by men, amongst other things because she became confused with the natural world. Of course, we do not have to enter into an opposition between sameness and difference. A cultivation of difference requires a cultivation of sameness. This cultivation needs a greater availability, generosity and awakening of the mind. It is also more fertile in energy, creation and happiness – for ourselves and for those who surround us – on the condition that we have not confused the same and the different nor substituted a stage for another in the relations.

M.S.: Can you elaborate on what you mean when you describe self-experience as intersubjective? Can you describe the difference between 'vertical' and 'horizontal' transcendence?

L.I.: From the very beginning, we live in relation with the other(s). Our first, even unconscious, self is relational. We would not exist without having made up a relational world with our mother. This relationship is not intersubjective strictly speaking: we are not yet two subjects in a certain way, but we already are two subjective worlds in relation with one another. And we did not know an experience of the self which was not somehow intersubjective. If we have not understood that – as is too often the case in our patriarchal tradition – we cannot reach a true relation between subjects. Our culture talks little about intersubjectivity. Nevertheless, our self-experience in any case remains intersubjective, and it is all the more so that we do not recognize the first other who took part in our world. Our self-experience is also always intersubjective because we share a culture, a tradition, a world constructed by many subjects. This sharing does not yet amount, however, to reaching intersubjectivity as a relation between two subjects belonging to different subjective worlds beyond a consciousness of the self which allows an opening to the other as such.

M.S.: Can you elaborate on a question you ask in 'Introducing: Love between us': 'What is spirit if it forces the body to comply with an abstract model that is unsuited to it?' (*I Love to You*, p. 25). What is the 'abstract model' you are referring to?

L.I.: The Western cultural model seems, most of the time, to obey abstract principles or ideas with respect to the body. Reaching an intelligible level then implies relinquishing the sensibility, which is linked up to the body. Even sensory perceptions are not cultivated in the West as a possible way of making the mind and the self blossom. But it is not only in the West, I am afraid, that spirit forces the body to submit to abstract models. All the neuter, so-called neutral, models are abstract, and the scientific and technological world, which is henceforth ours, risks rendering abstraction the most universal model which imposes its law on us.

M.S.: You've returned, in several works, to the image of the Buddha taking in the scent of a flower. What is the significance of this image for you?

L.I.: I laughed when reading your question. I wrote about Buddha looking at the flower, but not 'taking in the scent of a flower'. Probably I read something about that, but I cannot give you the exact reference. I can say that I experienced it during a summer. The question of looking at and contemplating is also present in *The Yoga Sutras of Patañjali*. But Patañjali often speaks about objects, material or mental, and about the necessity of overcoming the subject–object duality. From a masculine point of view it is fitting to surmount this duality, because it generally corresponds to an inability of the subject to stay in the self. Looking at a flower is different. The flower as such is not absolutely necessary for me to remain in myself. But it can help me because it is autonomous with respect to me, and it is also a living being. Thus I can concentrate and contemplate looking at a flower. And I can reach in this way a state of energy close to that described by Patañjali without for all that having to remove the flower as such. Furthermore, this state is linked with life, and allows one to reach an en-stasis in oneself while intensely living. It also permits an easier passage from a state of contemplation, even sometimes of culmination, to relations with other living beings, with other(s), with daily existence.

M.S.: You write that, thanks to a cultivation of breath and through a rebirth, my body is no longer a body engendered by my parents; it is also the one that I give back to myself. This way of thinking about the body challenges traditional psychoanalytic thinking, by describing individuation not as that which occurs exclusively in relation to one's parents, but between one's self-image, one's body, one's breath and language.

L.I.: I would have preferred that you stopped your question with the words 'one's parents'. In fact, I am not sure that 'one's self-image' takes part in the rebirth, nor even language, except when it permits becoming awakened by a transformation of energy. It seems to me that all that rather has to become silence or only a help in this process of transformation. Now our way of perceiving our own image and our way of speaking generally paralyse such an energetic awakening more than they are able to accompany and support it. Of course, such opening to rebirth constrains the usual psychoanalytic thinking and practice to deeply modify their economy.

M.S.: How has your exploration of yoga and Eastern thought affected your clinical work?

L.I.: It is difficult for me to answer your question because the change has occurred gradually. I also think that my way of approaching psychoanalysis was ready to integrate Eastern elements. I always worked on the structure of discourse as a stasis of energy to which it is important to give movement again. You will see that in the texts that I wrote on the enunciation of hysterics and obsessives. It is only an example amongst the texts that I have written before beginning to practice yoga. I used very little a kind of interpretation which claims to double or name what the point was. My strategy was more dynamic, energetic and freeing – trying to allow the patients to discover their own paths, to become creative or creators with respect to their own existences. For me, a criterion of a good end of the course of treatment is the discovery by the patients of their own way of creating, whatever the creation is. I also think that an autonomous way of breathing is very important in the psychoanalytic relation, from the part of the two participants. It is the best means of undoing an artificial transfer of affects and an infantile pathological dependence.

M.S.: What is your personal experience of yoga study? Can you describe the process of integrating your intellectual work and life practice with your embodied exploration of the breath? How did you begin weaving the two together?

L.I.: My first teacher indicated to me from the very beginning readings which could accompany my practice. Thus I entered the tradition not only with gestures that I made in a blind way but also with texts which helped me to become familiar with another cultural perspective. For years, I did not perceive the changes in my manner of thinking which resulted from my practice. After about ten years, I noted that I really thought differently. And it is the case still today. It is difficult to express the difference in a few words. I could say that I feel a greater liberty in the unfolding of my thinking, and that my thoughts take place in a wider space, with words that I decide to use for their poetic or creative value and not for an appropriateness already fixed by cultural rules. I also try to express the real of an experience without merely repeating that which has been taught to me. Of course, these tendencies are already present in my first texts. But today they seem to traduce the real more than just expressing a personal creativity. In other words, I could say that the two dimensions are more closely tied in my actual way of thinking.

M.S.: Could you elaborate on the difference between a 'language of information' and a 'syntax of communication'? (*I Love to You*, p. 113).

L.I.: In my opinion, a language of information aims to pass on meanings already coded. Most of the time informing amounts to repeating notices already heard, or, at least, a truth already appeared. Unfortunately the privilege of information is largely promoted by the media, whose language of information is confused with language of communication. When I use the word 'communication', I rather allude to communicating between people, and not to transmitting information. Linguistically, one could say that the language of communication – always firstly dialogic – puts the accent on the present production of the meaning and on the creative character of a communication which takes into account the two protagonists of the exchange. I could add that, while passing on information presupposes that we belong to the same world and share the same codes, communicating rather refers to an exchange between two partners who can belong to different worlds and who try to express something of their difference(s) to one another.

M.S.: In your sharp and eloquent study of the term 'I love you', and your translation of that common statement into 'I love to you', you put an emphasis on 'to' as a 'guarantor of indirection'. Could you say more about what the word 'to' prevents in this context?

L.I.: I did not choose the English translation of *J'aime à toi* by myself, and I am not able to decide whether 'to' is the best term to translate 'à'. Without doubt, the French choice *J'aime à toi* is deliberately agrammatical, but it works well to signify that 'toi' (you) has not become an object for 'je' (I). The 'à' intends to transform the usual subject–object relation into a relation between two subjects – as in the French construction 'Je parle à toi' (I talk to you). Furthermore, in French, little children use the expression 'J'aime à toi' in order to emphasize the 'toi' (you). This expression also can intervene in the amorous language. The main purpose of the 'à' is to indicate a passage from the discourse and culture of only one subject remaining in only one world, to which the other is supposed to belong, towards a discourse and a culture of two subjects belonging to two different worlds – the basic paradigm of this difference taking place between masculine and feminine subjectivities.

M.S.: During recent study with Richard Freeman, he said that 'Yoga is about listening. When we listen, we give space for things to be as they are'. In *I Love to You* and *To Be Two* you meditate on the nature and quality of listening as a way of approaching the world as other, approaching what is other in the most respectful and non-violent way. Could you talk about the relationship between listening and non-violence (*ahimsa* in Sanskrit)?

L.I.: I agree with the words of Richard Freeman. I would add that it is not sufficient to listen, it is necessary that a space of silence lets the things, and above all the other, be as they are. It is strange that Richard Freeman uses the word 'things' in this sentence. Things do not speak nor make music. I wonder whether he does not use 'to listen' in a metaphoric way. If it is the case, I am afraid that 'to listen' does not really give space for things – and even more for the other(s) – being as they are, because a metaphoric frame removes them from their own being. It is necessary to let things and other(s) to exist, to grow, to blossom and to present themselves in a free space that we manage for their entering into presence. It is the condition for not submitting them to our own perspective and for avoiding transgressing the limits of their world, of their being – a violent gesture even if it is not always visible nor perceived at the time it happens. If I refer to the other(s), I can also say that when we do not listen to them, we prevent them from exhaling. We, thus, deprive them of breathing, that is to say, of living. Perhaps things themselves have a particular way of exhaling? It is undoubtedly true for all living beings.

M.S.: How does one move from treating the other as object to approaching the other as other? Can you describe the psychological process of moving from a subject–object relationship to one of subject–other?

L.I.: It is first a matter of approaching the other as a living being, and also of considering that the problematic of object has nothing to do with that of the other. For example, the object is necessary for masculine subjectivity to resolve the difficulty of relating with the mother. Confusing object with the other amounts to including the other in the necessities of one's own subjective construction; it is not yet a question about the other as such. In other words, one could say that 'object(s)' often correspond to our needs, material or psychic, while the other, at least when we become really adult, belongs to a world that is situated beyond our needs: to the world of desires. To approach the other as other requires that we overcome the level of needs, that we become capable of desire.

M.S.: In what way is the subject–other relationship non-dualistic?

L.I.: I think that that the subject–other relationship has to remain potentially dualistic in all its modalities. For example, if in a society or a community, we do not remain capable of a dualistic relation with each other, we meet with the other(s) in a horizon – politic, cultural, religious – that is not proper to them or to ourselves. Which means that I submit the other to a world that is not their world, I submit myself to a world that is not mine, or I submit the two to a third that does not really take part in the world of each of us. Now if one of us or the two are submitted to a world alien to him or her, we cannot enter into relation as other(s). We become submitted to the same culture, the same order, the same tradition, or one of us submits the other to one's own world. Of course, I am not speaking about the so-called dual relation with the mother but about a way of relating with the other in which each can remain faithful to one's own self while respecting that of the other.

M.S.: How is your use of the terms 'becoming' or 'to be' different than Jung's idea of individuation or Deleuze's concept of becoming?

L.I.: In a few words, I could say that 'becoming' in my work signifies to let what or who I am grow and blossom. It does not mean becoming another thing with respect to my own being, as it seems to be the case in Deleuze's discourse, for example, about 'becoming woman' or 'becoming animal'. I feel myself closer to Jung's discourse about individuation on the condition that it considers the fact that I am from birth a singular individual. But I have to keep, and even to conquer, this individuation in spite of an undifferentiation I meet with. 'Becoming woman' or 'becoming animal' appears to me as a search for undifferentiation, instead of overcoming it. Except if Deleuze suggests that he is a woman and an animal. In this case 'becoming' amounts to realizing a something that belongs to his identity, and not to becoming the someone he is. To completely answer your question, I would need to read or read again some of these two writers' works.

M.S.: Could you elaborate on the statement you make in the prologue of *To Be Two*, where you write, 'Who I am for you and who I am for me is not the same, and such a gap cannot be overcome?' (pp. 9–10).

L.I.: The way in which I relate to and with myself is not the same as the way the other relates to and with me. These ways take part in a process of self-affection which is peculiar to each one. If this process is not respected in its specificity, relating together becomes impossible. In this case, I use the other to affect myself or the other uses me to affect him or her, and we are no longer two. This specific way of affecting oneself makes us non-substitutable one for the other. Taking care about the other, then, cannot correspond to thinking or acting in the other's stead, but, on the contrary, to confirming the other in his, or her, own world and providing them with energy in order that they solve their problem(s) by themselves. I could say that the other and myself inhabit two different worlds, and that to remove someone from one's own world is to abolish the possibility of a relation between the 'I' and the 'you'.

M.S.: Can you describe the relationship between breathing, speaking and listening?

L.I.: Of course the relationship between breathing and speaking or listening varies according to cultures. In a tradition in which breathing is cultivated as such, the difference between the three is more perceptible, and also in a tradition in which utterance is more related to an economy of breath. Generally, as I already said, speaking corresponds more to exhaling and listening to inhaling. It could happen that the two, in particular listening, occur in a moment in which the breath is held within the self, that is, in a suspension of breathing which leaves a space free for the speech of the other to take place without any appropriation. Also speaking can occur in such a situation. One could imagine that it is the case in our culture, but I think that breathing is rather enclosed within meaning, at least a certain sort of breathing, which does not amount to the usual way of breathing of a living being. Breathing, then, is hanging on concepts or ideas that are supposed to maintain it at a mental level. From this in part results our division into body and spirit or soul. And also our belief in the immortality of soul or spirit – they are no longer breathing. This would deserve a more substantial comment, unfolding and questioning amongst other things about our dependence on a culture which imposes on us a certain way of breathing to supposedly become intelligent or spiritual.

M.S.: What do you mean when you suggest, for example in Chapters 4 and 5 of *To Be Two*, that Western philosophy has not cultivated sensory perceptions?

L.I.: For example, we read in the comments of *The Yoga Sutras of Patañjali* that cultivating sensory perceptions can be a way to have access to concentration or contemplation, and in other Eastern texts that listening to the song of the birds is a help for the one who is in search of one's spiritual path. In our tradition, sensible perception is removed from a philosophical path and, more generally, from a search of wisdom and spirituality. Of course music is sometimes recognized as having some value in such a journey, on the condition that the intention of the creator or the words of the song be directed to God, to some ideal or absolute. But music as such, as art in general, is considered secondary with respect to a training towards wisdom. Only recently, Nietzsche, as a philosopher, tried to return to art a crucial role in accomplishing being and thinking. This is also the case for Heidegger, who wonders about the kind of language which could express realities of nature itself or of other living beings. In Eastern traditions, thought is not separate from art and prayer, but it is not the case in our tradition. Probably for this reason, philosophers such as Nietzsche or Heidegger search for a new philosophical horizon in the Eastern tradition in order to escape our meta-physical order. I imagine that because I am a woman and I care about intersubjectivity, I consider a cultivation of sensible perception to be absolutely necessary to success in meeting together with respect for our difference(s) and attractions.

M.S.: To what extent do you think language acquisition reifies or even limits our consciousness of bodily experience and our construction of gender? Can you give some examples?

L.I.: Perhaps it is not always the case but it is in our tradition. We lack a language capable of expressing our bodily and sensible experiences. And it is all the more so for a woman since our language, our *logos*, has been elaborated by men in order to solve their subjective necessities and to be used in the exchanges between men. More generally, our logic claims to overcome bodily and gender dimensions in order to reach a discourse neutral (in this case, neuter), universal and abstract with regard to sensible and personal experiences. This can explain why acquiring such a language 'reifies or even limits our consciousness of bodily experiences and our construction of gender'. It is even worse because our language constrains us to consider bodily and gendered experiences strange to humanity as such. They would belong to a part of animality, a lack of human education, that we have to overcome to become a human adult. I worked a lot with children of various ages notably about their sexuate belonging (see, for example, *Chi sono io? Chi sei tu?* to which a chapter of *Le partage de la parole* alludes; translated as 'Towards a Sharing of Speech', in *Key Writings*). I observed that, because of a lack of language to express their feelings and communicate between them, children withdraw into themselves, and they become aggressive towards girls, if they are boys; or fall into depression and dependence, if they are girls. When I helped them to become conscious of their sexuate identity and to enter into dialogue with respect for their difference(s), they were enthusiastic and happy. They asked to continue this experience, even by coming to Paris in order to work with me. Once more, I could add that our education system is based on the necessities of masculine subjectivity and does not take into account enough the values of feminine subjectivity, which are yet to be recognized and cultivated. Such an education does not help boys themselves, because it does not lead them to communicate with the other(s) and encloses them in a world in which masculine stereotypes appear as the top of the culture.

M.S.: Has your experience with yoga influenced the ways in which you address the body in your own clinical work?

L.I.: I think that my practice of yoga has helped me to let a living third be between the patient and myself, in particular air. My knowledge of the culture of yoga also encouraged me to pay attention to the role that sensible perceptions can play to reach autonomy, happiness and better relations with the other(s). Thus I cared more about the relation between subjectivity and the body, and no longer thought that subjectivity is only a question of language. Thanks to a culture of sexual, or better sexuate, difference combined with yoga, I understood that a relation between two bodies does not amount to a fusional maternal empathy nor to an animal attraction, but that it is the question of two autonomous worlds which must seek how to enter into relation while remaining two, and how to create something other than only natural children. Of course, I took more interest in energy economy and in the manner in which body and words intertwine in one subject and between two subjects. My conviction that a cure does not consist in finding appropriate words to interpret a past thanks to a transference onto the psychoanalyst was also reinforced, and I became more and more convinced that the main point is to free energy, to make it possible for the patient(s) to construct, one could say to create, their future, either at the level of their own work and task, or at the level of the relation(s) with the other(s). I better understood that respecting sexuate difference between us is most of the time sufficient to regulate energy, and we do not need an abstract law to succeed in that.

Bibliography

Irigaray, Luce, *J'aime à toi: Esquisse d'une félicité dans l'Histoire* (Paris: Grasset, 1992); trans. Alison Martin as *I Love to You: Sketch for a Felicity Within History* (London and New York: Routledge, 1996).

—— *Chi sono io? Chi sei tu? La chiave per una convivenza universale* (Casalmaggiore: Biblioteca di Casalmaggiore, 1999).

—— *Être Deux* (Paris: Grasset, 1997); trans. Monique M. Rhodes and Marco F. Cocito-Monoc from the Italian *Essere Due* (Torino: Bollati Boringhieri, 1994) as *To Be Two* (London and New York: Athlone and Routledge, 2000).

—— *Entre Orient et Occident. De la singularité à la communauté* (Paris: Grasset, 1999); trans. Stephen Pluháček as *Between East and West: From Singularity to Community* (New York: Columbia University Press, 2001).

Le Partage de la parole (Special Lecture series 4; Oxford: European Humanities Research Centre, University of Oxford/Legenda, 2001); the chapter with the same title as translated as 'Towards a Sharing of Speech', in *Key Writings*, pp. 77–94.

—— *Luce Irigaray: Key Writings* (London and New York: Continuum, 2004).

Patañjali, *The Yoga Sutras of Patañjali* (trans. and commentary Swami Satchidananda; Yogaville, VA: Integral Yoga, 1990).

Varenne, Jean, *Les Upanishads du Yoga* (Paris: Gallimard, 1974).

Being-Two in Architectural Perspective

Conversation between

Luce Irigaray and Andrea Wheeler

Andrea Wheeler: I attended the talk of Luce Irigaray at the International Architectural Association in London in November 2000, 'How can we live together in a lasting way?' Luce Irigaray then set out, to a very large and attentive audience, how architects could care about relations between people, and particularly about love, through building. She explained that architects do not take into consideration sufficiently the question of 'the closeness with the other', above all an other who is different, in the home. And she explained how this problem is crucial for us being able to live together. One of her most innovative proposals was to rebuild the home, starting with two small one-room apartments, which would replace the conventional shared dining-room, lounge and bedroom in order to make room for what is one's own world and for closeness with the other, for the individual's singularity as well as for the foundation or re-foundation of a community, beginning with that of the couple or the family. She developed the idea of how each one-room apartment could be arranged according to the singularity of each person, especially that of a man and of a woman. This published talk (in *Key Writings*, pp. 123–33) contains really stimulating ideas for creation in dwelling and in building.

As a young architect myself, with an interest in how the concept of love relates to architecture, I want to draw the attention of architects to the importance of the work of Luce Irigaray for inspiring a new way of building and arranging a home. Of course, the texts of Luce Irigaray are already known in the architectural world, but not sufficiently, in my opinion, above all in relation to her specific proposals and reflections on dwelling as such. These reflections are in part linked to the lecture by Heidegger ('Building, dwelling, thinking', in *Poetry, Language, Thought*), a lecture that Luce Irigaray continues, having in mind a philosophy of two subjects and the manner of being two and dwelling in two. The purpose of this dialogue with Luce Irigaray is thus to build bridges between her and architects, and also to indicate some solutions to the Institution which, today, is worrying about the presence of women in the architectural profession.

Encouraging diversity or campaigning for equality are only partial solutions to cultivating human potential. Encouraging diversity through policy aimed towards Human Resources managers does not address how to foster an environment which sustains the value of diversity or difference. Whilst asking women architects to consider how to conceive better working conditions has some value for the problem, the question of sustaining diversity exceeds the issue of equal opportunity within the work place. In this respect, Luce Irigaray has been involved in many projects and with many women's groups responding to very similar problems.

* * *

ANDREA WHEELER: What do you think of the notion of 'diversity' with respect to 'difference', in particular difference between women and men – a key word in your thought?

LUCE IRIGARAY: To promote only diversity, as it is often the case in our times, runs the risk of remaining in an unchanged horizon with regard to the relations with the other(s). We then entrust this problem to customs, moral rules or religious feeling without questioning our culture about its capability of meeting with the other as such. Furthermore, we are unable to open ourselves all the time to others different from us. We need to return to ourselves, to keep and save our totality or integrity, and this is possible only in sexuate difference. Why? Because it is the most basic difference, this one which secures for each one bridge(s) both between nature and culture and between us. It is starting from this difference that the other sorts of otherness have been elaborated. And if someone would raise here the problem of races or generations, it could be answered that races and generations do not prevent sexual attraction and that the behaviours with respect to them result from an elaboration, or non-elaboration, of sexual attraction. This attraction is stronger than the difference between the bodies. And it is more spiritual in a way. It also arises firstly between two. It is more initial and fundamental than diversity and can explain it, while the contrary is not true. Diversity is a means today to escape the question of sexuate difference and to reduce or merge women's liberation in a past world in which woman had not yet discovered and affirmed her own cultural values.

A.W.: My own work, like the research proposed by 'Architects for change', has aimed to determine how the profession can respond to and sustain difference. In the terminology of the RIBA (Royal Institute of British Architects) statement: it has sought to investigate how architecture can cultivate human potential in a space free of harassment or unfair discrimination in which the human rights of all individuals are respected. However, my approach, unlike the work anticipated by 'Architects for change', has sought to investigate this issue through contemporary philosophy, in particular your own work and I have posed the question of women and architecture as an investigation of 'love'.

I have argued that valuing the creative potential which individuals from diverse backgrounds contribute to architecture has to explore the conflict between expectations imposed and the wealth of women's creative possibilities. Reading your work, I have come to understand the question of sustaining diversity, or more crudely of women and architecture, as one of how to live, that is as a philosophical and architectural question which also profoundly describes what is at stake for women in the architectural work place. Furthermore, I understand the question of how to live in your work as life in respect and cultivation of the other's 'love' or more concisely, perhaps, that of rethinking dwelling. The work of the architect, in this context, becomes one of cultivating the other's existence, or in both architectural and philosophical terms, their dwelling; albeit dwelling profoundly reconsidered. For example, you write: 'Currently there is a kind of *one* built on a division of labour, of goods, of discourse, a *one* which is merely an enslaving complementarity: yet, love cannot but be free . . . If the *one* of love is ever to be achieved, we have to discover the *two*' (*An Ethics of Sexual Difference*, pp. 66–67).

How do you relate 'life', 'love', 'dwelling' and the question of the other(s)?

L.I.: Living is originary being in relation(s), particularly with the other. We always fail to achieve this being-in-relation because we confuse this with dwelling in a same world, with sharing a common world. But this does not take into consideration the possible diversity of the worlds and, first of all, the difference between the world of a man and that of a woman, their different ways of dwelling. Our culture belonging above all to a masculine world, to subject women to such a culture is to conceal their subjectivity and thus destroy a possible being in relation(s) between men and women. Of course, they can partly compose an undifferentiated universe, a universe of 'somebodies' where relations do not really exist between people. These relations are supposed to be mediatized by the same world: the same things, the same language, the same values, the same home. However, this 'same world' does not exist without destroying the specific world in which each one lives. It is difficult to realize that we inhabit different worlds while apparently we share a common quotidian reality. But considering only this dimension, we already are forgetting the level of a being in relation(s) with respect for difference(s) – that is to say, a being in relation with the other as such. In order to leave a culture in which being with the other(s) only means to take part in the same world, we have to overcome an undifferentiated relation with respect to the other(s). 'Undifferentiated' here can be endowed at least with a double signification: without difference and indifferent, that is to say both unimportant and awakening no feeling, perhaps not even any specific mood. The other is then confused with a general mood towards the world, the world to which I belong and that I feel as mine. In order to meet with the other as such, we have to reverse the situation: to leave our usual quotidian in order to open ourselves to the strange, the still unknown, the unusual and unfamiliar. We have to give the precedence to the other and not to our usual world. This way of thinking and building could be more fitting for women, in particular architects. The discourse of girls and female adults bears witness to that. And I cannot agree with the fact that this could result only from a feminine alienation, as I have sometimes heard. But, of course, this priority given to the relation to and with the other – and not the others as an undifferentiated people – needs to be thought and cultivated: it cannot remain at the level of a simple mood or feeling.

A.W.: Thinking dwelling as love in architecture also has some personal motive for me, foreseeing the call for research by 'Architects for change', and trying to understand difficulties I have had of being a woman and an architect. Within the Institution through social convention, women, and men, can feel obliged to adopt masculine modes of identity conceived as authoritarian. Women, in particular, are continuously asked to accommodate themselves to contradictory male expectations. Conforming to unspoken and unwritten conventions can place women in untenable positions; but attempting to interpret the difficulties faced within the Institution – especially when the effects of patriarchy can be concealed and invidious – can also lead to conflict, albeit a conflict that reveals the tension between recognizing the cultural construction of identity and the need to find one's own path. Thinking love is a way of understanding my own personal desire to live, create or build in my own way outside the horizons of family expectations; which includes a wider social family and the models of femininity it presents. As you write in your paper 'How Can We Live Together in a Lasting Way?'

> Intimacy, familiarity, and proximity do not exist only through living alongside one another and sharing the same space. On the contrary, that often leads to their destruction. The intimate and the familiar are first confused with being in the mother, being with the mother, and dwelling in the family home. But this perception of proximity is then mixed with, or even reduced to an infantile need for undifferentiation, whereby that which seems close belongs to the parental or genealogical universe, sheltering a child's birth and becoming . . . In order to conquer and affirm her or his particular being and becoming, the subject must renounce this initial experience of the familiar. (*Key Writings*, pp. 132–33)

One of the more beneficial ways to address problems of women within the architectural institution, you suggest, has to be criticism directed towards society and socio-economic factors, including their predetermining myths, with the creation of positive alternative fictions, myths or 'love stories'. I have found some of your re-evaluations, in particular that of Aphrodite and her love rethought, as influential. Aphrodite, in my opinion, describes a mode of being for the woman architect, who cultivates being-two.

Could you say a little more here about your thinking and path towards 'love'?

L.I.: My first step on the path of my liberation as woman was criticism. I had to leave a culture of a single subject in which thinking, loving and even living were not possible for me. My first books – *Speculum* and *This Sex Which Is Not One*, for example – testify to this attempt to go out of the prison of a tradition in which I had to conform to models which were not suitable for me as woman. But to remain in criticism was no more appropriate to my desire of living, loving and thinking. Criticism ought to remain a scientific attitude and not a basic and exclusive behaviour. I knew that my way of loving and thinking was mistaken and had thus to discover how to live, love and think after leaving a monosexuate culture. The unfolding of my work bears witness to this quest. I sought new mediations to differ from the so-called neutral culture in which I was merged – be they genealogy, language, law, religion, and so on. These mediations were a means of differentiating myself without remaining only in a critical attitude. They represented a positive means of going along my own path. Next I tried, and still now am trying, to discover or create mediations between paths which are different. I understood that, to reach this, I had to start from sexuate difference, that is to say from the most basic and universal difference, a difference founded both in nature and in culture and which crosses all history(ies), tradition(s) and people(s). To work on this difference represents a difficult task, a task that cannot remain only mental, as our culture has taught us, but which requires a participation of the whole of ourselves, a sort of conversion of ourselves. Throughout this journey, I wanted and needed to continue to love in order to remain alive, creative by myself and happy, even if the path was very difficult.

A.W.: Your approach to dwelling differs considerably from other contemporary philosophers, in particular Heidegger who is more familiar amongst architects. However, whilst Heidegger does not gender his mode of existence, in *The Age of the Breath* you suggest that women's task is not, firstly, to make a world – which is more associated with a male and also perhaps an architectural behaviour – but to cultivate an autonomous being, an interiority, even in being-two. You write that 'The feminine is not called to carry out the task of constructing a world which is similar to man's . . . To become a world herself, to cultivate herself without violence or power over what surrounds her – all of these correspond more to the feminine to be' (*To Be Two*, p. 72).

In addition, the cultivation of the 'to be' of woman may also be capable of redirecting man to his own 'to be'. In this respect, being-two in architecture could differentiate the role and function of the architect. And that could favour an autonomous existence for women. For example, you write in 'How can we live together in a lasting way?'

> Living an existence of one's own requires an awareness of one's own specific world, whose contents and limits must be recognized and

> affirmed. Only beyond these contents and limits can the other be encountered, desired and loved, provided that his or her own world is respected, and without infringing its frontiers. Proximity can be created because of the limits with which each one, the masculine or the feminine subject, surrounds their own particular universe. It constitutes a third place beyond the maintaining of each one's own world, a place that belongs to no one but to the two . . . This place remains always open – which does not mean simply empty – for a possible welcoming of the other. (*Key Writings*, p. 133)

How could you link the work of constructing outside oneself – as it is often the case for a man – and the work of becoming a world oneself, of building oneself?

L.I.: Generally to build is understood as building something with material(s) to which it is given form(s). These views on building are rather masculine. From the beginning of our Western culture, man has tried to differ from nature by mastering this, which provides raw material, with his technique and technology. Building, then, implies to cut oneself off from nature, including human nature, especially represented as mother but even as woman. Building is seldom understood as building oneself with respect for the nature that we are. This way of building, nevertheless, is in some way asked of woman, notably in engendering and loving. To engender and to assure motherhood require a culture of oneself as nature, and it is also true in order to awake and sustain sexual desire. This way of building herself as nature is not sufficient because it is in the greatest part imposed on the woman by an other. To reach building herself, woman has to preserve and cultivate her nature also in an autonomous and decided manner. She has to discover how to pass from her material or bodily nature to a cultural or spiritual nature appropriate to her. That is to say that she has to discover how to live, to love, to speak, to think in accordance with her nature. Building a home must entail a concern for raw or transformed material through projects, technique and technology. But could an architect build houses for others if he, or she, is not capable of building their self? Unfortunately this dimension, the most important dimension in building, is often neglected, and even forgotten. Again today I listened to an interview with architects, and the novelty that they proposed was to manage a space for the car in the flat itself. They were very serious, discussing how much this novelty could improve the life of people. I said to myself that probably their project would be successful because it takes place in a system in which we already are. In this system, few architects wonder about the necessary relation between building a house and building oneself, at least at the level of being and not only having, possessing. If it was the case, the question of how to live together, how to dwell in two, would awake their attention more than how to welcome the car into the flat.

A.W.: 'How Can We Live Together in a Lasting Way?', as already cited, suggests that the architect and architecture is in a privileged position to provide a means of sustaining this mode of existence. It also suggests that architecture should reconsider the issue of existence or dwelling in order to correspond to the reality of two (sexes). You say:

> The issue of dwelling presents us with complex problems, which an architect should take into consideration. It is one of enabling the human subject to subsist, to exist and to be, to become – while most often being two, or more than two. Yet those who design dwellings are primarily concerned with subsistence: shelter, recuperation through eating and sleeping, provision of basic hygiene. (*Key Writings*, p. 123)

Identifying dwelling as an issue that the architect should reconsider, whilst it corresponds to Heidegger's arguments in 'Building, dwelling, thinking' also 'implies a need to think about possible ways of coexisting within the same residence without destroying the respective subjectivities' (*Key Writings*, p. 124). However, living to be two has as yet evaded architectural discourse, but recent theorists have sought to take up your work to suggest its value for contemporary theory. Some women and men may be wilfully blind to the problems you want to consider, while a number of women architects, who have an interest in your philosophy, have also begun to suggest that your work offers an important challenge to contemporary architectural theory. Responding to this interest in being-two by theorists, to this desire for such a discourse, must also be one aspect of an ethical practice approaching being-two.

How and if I can discover or rediscover feminine values in architecture, perhaps more simply, the question of how to live, or love, has occupied many years of my architectural education. Initially my interest in your philosophy was motivated by Elizabeth Grosz's introductions to your work, in particular her paper 'Women, *chora*, dwelling' (*Architecture and the Feminine*, pp. 22–27) and the paper that she cites 'Où et comment habiter?'(*Cahiers du Grif*, pp. 139–43). Grosz's paper has also motivated a number of other women architects to discuss your work in terms of *un lieu propre*, a space of one's own. You have suggested that the need for 'a space of one's own' should not merely evoke the request Virginia Woolf made in her time for a 'room of her own' but rather a criticism of conventional understandings of 'space' within patriarchal traditions, with a call for a heart of one's own, a soul of one's own, a form of interiority (*Le partage de la parole*, pp. 46–47). This space is necessary, in your opinion, because: 'there is no doubt that competitiveness and fighting will undermine the communal life. Besides, if so-called communal life is forced upon us and not truly shared, is it any wonder people seek love affairs outside the home?' ('How Can We Live Together in a Lasting Way?', in *Key Writings*, p. 127).

In the recent publication *Le Partage de la parole* you also write that being-two expresses the need to construct a relationship with the other as belonging to a different world. In fact, the world would not be one but at least two – two worlds corresponding to the two sexes or genders with their own languages. Thus, similarly critical of theorists who have described your method in terms of mimicry, the poetic – *poietic* – of being-two, you suggest, is in part, as yet, outside language and as such has to be cultivated. In this respect, nature plays an important role in sustaining difference. This difference, you insist, is not simply biological or social, but a question of difference in relational identity. Moreover, you write:

> Maintaining the diversity of worlds enables and obliges one's return to oneself, but also allows her or him to become familiar with the world of the other, not only at the level of words and ideas but also through everyday perception. ('How Can We Live Together in a Lasting Way?', in *Key Writings*, p. 130)

Could you say a little more about the problem of the 'different worlds'? In my opinion it is very crucial to your work but it is also difficult to understand because it is new thought.

L.I.: Most of the time, we think of our relations with the other(s) inside a single and same world. We now discover that it is not as simple as we thought, for example through the difficulty of coexistence between peoples, cultures. Even then many consider that the solution to diversity is to integrate the other(s) – the foreigner(s) – in their own country. This could be democratically possible only thanks to the definition of a new legislation which would take into consideration the persons as such and not only the properties or the goods, be they material or spiritual. In this case coexistence becomes possible, and integration useless. But we are still at the level of a very minimum, a level indispensable but not sufficient. We have not yet resolved the problem of the difference of subjectivities due to the culture. Architects could care about that by allowing different cultures or worlds to be respected inside the house, the flat. Perhaps through the question of multiculturalism, many people, including architects, could understand the necessity of worrying about difference when dwelling or building houses or flats. But the question, there, above all concerns diversity – that is to say, a multiple of the one: humanity as man or neuter individual. It is more difficult to make clear that difference exists, first of all and in a universal way, between man and woman, men and women. Of course they partly inhabit a same world, be it nature or a historically constructed world. But if there exists an objectivity of the world which surrounds them, they subjectively live it in another way. First, there are men who generally have built the world, a world appropriate to them, and through which they ruled over nature itself, hence men and women cannot dwell in it in the same way. Second, as analysis of language clearly shows, the relational identities of men and women are not the same. They differently live and express the relation to themselves, to the other(s), to the world. They thus dwell in different worlds, even if certain aspects of these worlds seem, and sometimes are, objectively alike. All of us, and particularly architects, have to take into account the difference between the worlds in which each dwells, and have both to allow their existence and becoming and to care about the coexistence with the other, in respect for difference(s).

A.W.: The fundamental opposition between nature and culture is rethought in being-two, so that the female subject does not constitute herself in opposition to nature but by means of nature:

> Nature represents to some extent the special and preferred instrument of female becoming, an instrument which merges with the self and is not external to the self as it often is for the male . . . It is a question of coming to terms with nature in a fashion which is not domination but measure,

> rhythm, harmony, growth, fecundity. ('Une identité relationnelle différente', trans. Andrea Wheeler, in Le Partage de la parole, p. 46)

In addition: '*Nature has a sex*, always and everywhere. All traditions that remain faithful to the cosmic order have a sex and take account of natural powers (*puissances*) in sexual terms. They are also regulated by *alternations* that do not truly contradict each other' (*Sexes and Genealogies*, p. 108).

For Heidegger, conceptions of nature correspond philosophically with the question of being and Being; but being-two approaches the question of being and Being differently, taking into account the dimension of the sexual, or better sexuate, difference. How could you take this into consideration when building a space to live?

L.I.: As I wrote in the text 'How Can We Live Together in a Lasting Way?', it is important to assure in the house a presence of nature. It preserves the relation with a living universal, a universal that can be shared by all people and that provides a bridge between them, in particular between woman and man. This presence of nature in the home can be experienced by each one according to one's own identity and thus favours a relation with respect for difference(s). Such a presence can also be a help, for each one and between the two, to pass from body to soul, to love, to words, notably thanks to an elaboration of air through breathing. Then, each can keep their own economy, and thus coexistence is possible in difference(s). Nature offers a mediation that a constructed or fabricated world does no longer provide – a mediation inside each self, a mediation between the two, and also a mediation between the house and the universe as cosmos. This mediation constitutes the basis for a relation amongst all people, not only the neighbourhood and people of the same country or culture but people of a global society. It would be possible here to evoke the fourfold of Heidegger. But it already represents a construction in relation to the four elements of the universe, to which the return seems necessary as such, in order to elaborate a being-two in the respect for difference between masculine and feminine subjectivities, notably in the way of relating with nature itself.

A.W.: You have criticized architects for not thinking difference in a fitting way. Moreover, you suggest that the traditional representation of difference forces those who live within it into immobilizing stereotypes that prevent them from existing, becoming and meeting with the other. The play of stereotypes certainly does not allow an environment free of unfair discrimination or where human potential can be cultivated. As an alternative you suggest:

> The horizontal transcendence between the sexes creates space, spaces, whereas reducing it to a genealogy destroys them or at least fills them up. Of course spaces opened up by difference cannot figure directly in a home because they cannot be represented. However, they can be evoked and raised by maintaining and reawakening difference in the way of dwelling. ('How Can We Live Together in a Lasting Way?', in *Key Writings*, p. 132)

Being-two is another approach to difference than that thought through the work of Derrida who has been a popular philosopher amongst architects.

What do you think about the stereotypes related to sexual difference? How could we pass from them to your thought of sexual, or rather sexuate, difference?

L.I.: When we speak about stereotypes, notably those related to sexual, or sexuate, difference, it is often as if they were imposed on us only from the outside by a society or a culture. Of course this is partly the case, but it does not explain when and how stereotypes were born. When I carried out the work with children on education towards a citizenship respectful of difference(s), I noted that stereotypes arise amongst children themselves. The most fertile time for the root of these stereotypes is when they are ten years old. In my opinion, stereotypes are not only imposed from the outside on the children, they come above all from a lack of education concerning their sexuate identity, their sexuate difference, their sexual attraction. For example, if this attraction remains uncultivated, it runs the risk of becoming a withdrawal into oneself for each sex which creates stereotypes. These are then shared amongst those who belong to the same gender. They often express an aggressiveness which has connection with an unsatisfied attraction and the frustration resulting from that. To help the children to not fall back in stereotypes requires an education of their own subjectivity and about the means of entering into relations with respect for difference(s). The children really like such an education because it takes into account their real being and their wish for relations between them. Furthermore such a training represents a way of passing from instinct to love, from blind attraction to a desire respectful towards the other. To prevent the birth of stereotypes in education in fact corresponds to a means of reaching a humanity more fulfilled, happy, and capable of a transcendental feeling fruitful in creating, here and now, notably spaces suitable for dwelling.

A.W.: If dwelling, or being-two, can be thought as a cultivation of the love, exploring being-two in architecture creates the possibility of a place of love, dwelling, hospitality, creativity, notably in communication and talking. This opens ways of thinking about how to cultivate and sustain difference within the work place.

I understand your *at least two* – for example, *two lips* – as a poetic construction in language, perhaps one of the best known amongst architects, which acts to sustain this new dwelling, 'where we come to relearn ourselves and each other, in order to become women, and mothers, again and again' (*And the One Doesn't Stir Without the Other*, p. 67). Your changes to the habits of language with the *at least two lips* build a threshold to a new mode of being and Being. However, sustaining these modifications in language is a collective project, again of at least two. In *And the One Doesn't Stir Without the Other*, the title suggests both that we do not move together and that it is only together that we can move. This could mean thinking love so as to stir the other up, liberating the two: mother and daughter, another sort of being-two: 'Making from your gaze an airy substance to inhabit and shelter me from our resemblance' (*And the One Doesn't Stir Without the Other*, p. 67). 'Breath', 'perception' and a 'sensible transcendental' ought to sustain being-two, you say. In architecture, the place of the elemental, the place of the hearth are to be rethought. But not only them. Another hearth has to be born from the cultivation of the attraction and desire between two:

> Pornographic representations can arouse sexual desire in a punctual way and, for their effect to become durable, the intensity of the stimulation has to be constantly increased. But even then, instead of maintaining desire, they eradicate it, subjecting it to tools and techniques exterior to the subject.
>
> It is rather through a process of internalization by each one that the spacing and the space for welcoming the other should be elaborated. Obviously these spaces cannot be reduced to some equivalents of a womb or to some evocations of the vagina, for that would risk lapsing

again into complementarity or genealogy, without attaining to create space that opens transcendence between the sexes.

Hereafter, it is the difference itself that will guarantee a passage between earth and sky. The air it provides between her and him is animated by fire and currents, by winds, by desire, with a movement going from one to the other, as well as from the lowest to the highest of the body and the universe, from the most material to that which is most subtle in the micro- and macrocosm.

The centre of a residence is no longer simply the traditional hearth. ('How Can We Live Together in a Lasting Way?', in *Key Writings*, p. 132)

How could I use your proposals about 'at least two', 'breath', 'perception' and 'sensible transcendental' in a collective project?

L.I.: You seem to confuse the two of 'two lips' and the two of 'being-two' as persons. Now the expression 'two lips' tries to express a basic way of self-affection for the feminine subject, while 'being-two' refers to a relation between two subjects. Self-affection is a determining factor in reaching 'being-two' but cannot amount to relation itself. Turning one's attention or one's feeling only to 'the two lips' remains in the perspective of one and alone subject. Of course this subject now is in the feminine but we have not yet reached a culture of two subjects. Often people who speak about 'feminine difference' forget that it does not yet correspond to the difference between two subjects, one masculine and one feminine, being in relation. The meaning of the word 'transcendental' can change according to the two ways of understanding the word 'difference'. A 'sensible transcendental' could exist in the first case, but to remain in a single and proper world prevents us from perceiving the transcendental to which I refer when speaking of the difference 'between' two subjects. This point is important to save and lay out the space for living together: the space for each one and the space between the two. Woman needs a space where gathering with herself and her self-affection are favoured. The 'two lips' and, in part, the 'sensible transcendental' rather have a share in the space for her, while 'being-two' must take into account the two spaces, the passage between them and the world built together. Another point: as said in 'How can we live together in a lasting way?', perceptions would be kept alive by the preservation of two different worlds. Which prevents perceptions from falling asleep in the familiarity of a unique world or in a neuter context, a context built without caring about perceptions, all perceptions: visual, but also tactile, auditory, olfactory, gustatory. Architects ought to think about spaces which appeal to all our perceptions – through forms, matter, colour, sounds, odours, and so on – and in a way that is suitable for each self-affection in their own rooms. About a culture of breathing, I have already recalled the need to allow a place for nature in the home, and to save a place of intimacy with oneself, that is to say, for each way of breathing, each breath, including in its relation to the transcendental.

A.W.: Contemporary feminism in architectural theory, where it proposes itself as a new discourse has, on occasion, undervalued the work of women in architecture who have associated themselves, or have been associated with feminism, proposing a concern for difference in opposition to feminism. Although you do not use the term feminism – that is 'a word ending with -ism' – preferring to it the term 'women's liberation', you do suggest that understanding the culturally problematic mother–daughter relationship (rethought for example through the myth of Demeter and Kore, Aphrodite or Hestia) is one of the most difficult task for women working within feminist contexts and can contribute to difficulties in sustaining a continued discourse amongst women. In your interviews with women, and also men, in *Why Different?*, you write that we need to free our mothers with ourselves. Thus, 'being-two' addresses not only the question of initiating and sustaining diversity within the work place. 'Being-two' addresses a problematic discourse of feminism in architecture, of gender theory and architecture, and of women amongst themselves within the profession.

Architecture as a means of being-two thus becomes a reformulation of the question of existence(s), being in the world, being with others or dwelling. Moreover, what is significant in thinking dwelling as being-two is that it exceeds contemporary discourses on gender and architecture that your work is more often associated with.

You have already largely answered to an undifferentiated perspective in dwelling as being in the world, being with the other(s). In your view, how could this be accomplished in architecture?

L.I.: Being in relation as two, in a horizontal harmonious way, is the means of emerging from all sorts of undifferentiations: with nature, with mother as origin, with those of the same people. This cannot be imposed on us from the outside but has to be elaborated by ourselves through caring about a relation in two respectful for difference(s). Of course the question does not concern a quantitative difference, which somehow remains in sameness and maintains relations in a parental or hierarchical dimension, and even in a sadomasochistic bond. Reciprocity between the two then does not exist, a reciprocity necessary to emerge from undifferentiation, while it is not the same that each can give to the other because of the difference between them. Most of the time, feminists unfortunately have not taken sufficiently into consideration the necessity of differing, from nature but also from oneness, to gain their feminine autonomy. Furthermore many still think of their liberation in terms of becoming similar to men, directly or indirectly, through possessing the same goods, the same rights, the same possibilities in general. It is a new way to return to undifferentiation, an undifferentiation worse than that with nature because it is artificial and without worthwhile resources for the self. Such an undifferentiation constitutes a possible humus or grounding for all kinds of totalitarianisms. Of course the matter is not to oppose a social equality to a traditional hierarchical difference but to understand that reaching a real equality, or rather a real equivalence, of rights for both man and woman, requires us to consider difference between them and not to reduce or assimilate the one to the other. Which would amount to the most radical and irreparable inequality.

A.W.: In architecture, being-two could thereby be thought in terms of the relationship between woman (or man) and nature, and this could be a concern for architects interested in sustainability or in philosophies of dwelling – as in your poetic prologue of *To Be Two*. Being-two could be thought in terms of the relationship between man and woman – as in *I Love To You*, *To Be Two* and *The Way of Love* – which should be of interest for architects who care about gender or feminism, albeit this way of thinking feminism has more to do with rethinking democracy. What sort of encounter can initiate an approach to being-two within architecture and how this can be sustained, nevertheless, remains a question for me. In Australia, I presented a paper about an imagined dialogue with Luce Irigaray, before a real dialogue with Luce Irigaray became possible. It was an imagined relationship which sought to question how to cultivate being-two in architecture. The question you have already asked me: How can we build bridges between two in architecture? (see *Dialogues*, p. 115) is one that I have continued to think about.

Could you suggest some examples of practicing being-two in architecture, notably with a democratic perspective in view?

L.I.: I already suggested some means when giving a talk at the International Architectural Association of London a few years ago, as the text 'How can we live together in a lasting way?' shows. For example, instead of centering the house around a dining room and a bathroom – which are functional and undifferentiated spaces which assimilate the couple or the family into a collective unity founded on a loss of individual identity – why not rebuild the residence starting with two small one-room apartments which would replace the common dining room and bedroom? This spatial topography would make room – in the same space – for each and one's own world, and thus favours closeness with the other without falling back into undifferentiation. Dwelling could then preserve the individual's singularity as well as allow a refoundation of a community, beginning with the community of the couple or the family. After analyzing many samples of the respective languages of man and woman, I could suggest to architects to give more place in her apartment than in his to relational life, to the relationship between two, to difference, sexuate difference in particular. This could be achieved in different ways. For example, the area for receiving the other would be more visible in her room than in his: a large bed covered with cushions for her and a futon for him, or a lounge area for relaxing together and chatting for one and, for the other, a bar for sharing a drink without the relational aspect being too immediately obvious. The space for working will be less neutral in her apartment, which does not signify that her work is less valuable but that it is not a substitute for relational life. Also, women and men do not appreciate materials, forms and colours in the same way. Men generally prefer metallic and shiny matter, women materials that are warmer to look and to touch. Women would favour rounded forms and men angular forms. Moreover, according to experiments I have carried out with colours amongst boys and girls, the world of each one is also different in that respect, and it would be fitting to take this into account when caring about paint, carpets, bedding and other decorative aspects of each small apartment. These are some initial suggestions to stimulate creativity in order to allow a being and dwelling as two with respect for each singularity and world, which is a condition for desiring and loving in a lasting way.

A.W.: The cultivation of breath and of perception, both means by which you have suggested we can approach being-two, have correspondences with more Eastern traditions. Heidegger's work also has a relation with Eastern philosophies. Levinas's work has a relation to the Kabbalistic traditions, and love, in Levinas, is thought as a relationship to a sensible other, whilst an ethical relationship is reserved for a transcendental Other. Thus, Levinas distinguishes the sensible and the transcendental in a way that conforms to the tradition of Western thought. For Heidegger, care is more fundamental than love, a way of understanding ourselves as being in the world, and being with others. Like Levinas, Heidegger approaches his influences from firmly within the Western tradition. Both these philosophies you reconsider from your own understanding of love. I understand your approach to love amongst other things as reworking the distinction of sensible and transcendental of the Western tradition. It is a way of rethinking the properties of feminine identity. Reconstruction of subjectivity needs to be a collective project. This is the problem I have with rethinking feminism in architecture, and approaching being-two.

How could I join, and already think together, a collective work starting from your being-two?

L.I.: For me there is no opposition between a collective work and my proposals about being-two. The project concerning coexistence in difference that I present in 'How Can We Live Together in a Lasting Way?' could be adopted and promoted by a group of architects having in mind to build or to transform council houses. Perhaps a certain idea of democracy prevents some people from being in agreement with my perspective. Democracy can be understood as reduction of all people to individuals sharing a common undifferentiated (co)existence and discourse. Or democracy can be understood as an opportunity for each one to live one's own singularity. To attain and enjoy such a possibility, we must, all the time, consider and preserve the difference between us, starting from between us as two. If we do not do that, we fall again into an anonymous community of people in which we lose our subjectivity, our desire, our happiness. I think that neither Heidegger nor Levinas have envisioned this problem with a sufficient attention. For example, if I project transcendence only into the Other and do not preserve it, at every moment, between the other and myself, such a transcendence will correspond to an absolute singularity or to the ideal or Absolute of a people – which, in a way, could amount to a sort of anonymity and runs the risk of a fundamentalism closed to all sorts of other. As for the 'care' of Heidegger,

I am afraid that it is too neutral and anonymous to take into consideration the other as such – the other here present with myself in an apparent same space or time but who, in fact, belongs to another world. This configuration is at stake when we meet with a foreigner, but, even more radically, with the sexuate different other. To forget and neglect this one in collective projects amounts to making life, desire and coexistence impossible for each one. This ought not to be a democratic ideal.

Bibliography

Grosz, Elizabeth, 'Women, *chora*, Dwelling', *Architecture and the Feminine: Mop up Work* (special issue of *ANY: Architecture New York* 1/4; ed. Jennifer Bloomer; January/February 1994), pp. 22–27.

Heidegger, Martin, 'Building, dwelling, thinking', trans. Albert Hofstadter, in *Poetry, Language, Thought* (New York: Harper and Row, 1971[1954]), pp. 145–61.

Irigaray, Luce, *Et l'une ne bouge pas sans l'autre* (Paris: Editions de Minuit, 1979); trans. Helene Wenzel as 'And the One Doesn't Stir Without the Other', in *Signs, French Feminist Theory*, 7/1 (1981): 56–59.

—— 'Où et comment habiter?', *Cahiers du Grif* (24 March 1983), pp. 139–43.

—— *Speculum. De l'autre femme* (Paris: Minuit, 1974); trans. Gillian C. Gill as *Speculum: Of the Other Woman* (Ithaca, NY: Cornell University Press, 1985).

—— *Ce sexe qui n'en est pas un* (Paris: Minuit, 1977); trans. Catherine Porter with Carolyn Burke as *This Sex Which is Not One* (Ithaca, NY: Cornell University Press, 1985).

—— *Éthique de la différence sexuelle* (Paris: Editions de Minuit, 1984); trans. Carolyn Burke and Gillian C. Gill as *An Ethics of Sexual Difference* (Ithaca, NY and London: Cornell University Press and Continuum, 1993).

—— *Sexes et parentés* (Paris: Editions de Minuit, 1987); trans. Gillian C. Gill as *Sexes and Genealogies* (New York: Columbia University Press, 1993).

—— *J'aime à toi: Esquisse d'une félicité dans l'Histoire* (Paris: Grasset, 1992); trans. Alison Martin as *I Love to You: Sketch for a Felicity Within History* (London and New York: Routledge, 1996).

—— *Le temps du souffle* (Rüsselsheim: Christel Göttert Verlag, 1999); trans. Katja van de Rakt, Staci von Boeckman and Luce Irigaray as *The Age of the Breath* (includes also the German and Italian versions of the text).

—— *Why Different? A Culture of Two Subjects* (interviews with Luce Irigaray), ed. Luce Irigaray and Sylvère Lotringer, trans. Camille Collins, Peter Carravatta, Ben Meyers, Heidi Bostic, Stephen Pluháček from the French or the Italian (New York: Semiotext(e), 2000).

—— *Être Deux* (Paris: Grasset, 1997); trans. Monique M. Rhodes and Marco F. Cocito-Monoc from the Italian *Essere Due* (Torino: Bollati Boringhieri, 1994) as *To Be Two* (London and New York: Athlone and Routledge, 2000).

—— *Le Partage de la parole* (Special Lecture series 4; Oxford: European Humanities Research Centre, University of Oxford/Legenda, 2001).

——*Dialogues Around Her Work*, special issue of *Paragraph* 25.3 (Edinburgh: Edinburgh University Press, 2002).

—— *The Way of Love* (London and New York: Continuum, 2002); trans. Heidi Bostic and Stephen Pluháček from the French *La Voie de l'Amour* (not yet published).

—— 'Comment habiter durablement ensemble?', trans. Alison Martin, Maria Bailey and Luce Irigaray as 'How Can We Live Together in a Lasting Way?' in *Luce Irigaray: Key Writings*, pp. 123–33.

Becoming Woman, Each One and Together

Conversation between

Luce Irigaray and Gillian Howie

Luce Irigaray: It is in the context of a conference around becoming divine in the feminine – University of Liverpool, Hope College and Department of Philosophy, June 2005 – that we met for the first time. We shared some interests and also friendship. We, thus, decided to continue working together. Sometimes it is the one who asks the other to be interviewed on occasion of the reprint of a book that she co-edited – cf. *Third Wave Feminism*, edited by Stace Gillis, Gillian Howie and Rebecca Munford – and sometimes it is the other who calls for a contribution to a conference and a book of which she takes charge – 'In All the World, We Are Always Only Two' (University of Nottingham, 23–25 June 2006) and *Luce Irigaray: Teaching*, edited by Luce Irigaray with Mary Green. In June 2007, the international annual seminar that one organizes for people doing their PhD on her work has been welcomed in the University of Liverpool, both by the Hope College and the Department of Philosophy of which the other was head, an other who, on her part, organized a day of international conference to conclude the seminar. What will be the future collaboration? I hope that our works and our lives will somehow continue to intertwine and to bear fruit and joy to each of us and to many others. For now, this is how our conversation went on:

*   *   *

GILLIAN HOWIE: Do you think that the wave metaphor is a helpful way to understand stages in feminist theory/the women's movement?

LUCE IRIGARAY: Is it really a metaphor or an image that tries to suggest an affinity of women with water, with fluid, with sea? If the stages in the feminist movement correspond to waves, this could suggest a moving ceaselessly without ever changing the bottom which supports such a movement. And also: that the movement is caused by things other than itself, by things in part external with respect to itself: a star outside it, the ground on which it takes place, etc. Thus, the matter would be of a permanent but instable and not autonomous movement which could never assume a definitive meaning or form. Waves in some way refer to a mythical time and not to historical times. How could we articulate mythical time with historical times? Certainly, it is a question that the entry of women into Western culture raises. And the problem is not to substitute a kind of temporality for another but to overcome this opposition and dichotomy.

G.H.: You have refused to belong to any one faction within the women's movement but continue to define yourself as a feminist. Can you explain why it is important to you to be a feminist rather than, say, a 'post-feminist'?

L.I.: Where did you see that I define myself as 'feminist'? On the contrary, I have many times protested against the fact that I could be called a feminist. I have repeated that I do not want to belong to any 'ism' category, be it feminism, post-feminism, post-modernism, etc. Other people designate me as feminist, but not myself. Perhaps because these words ending in 'ism' allude to something both too rigid and too evanescent. The relation between the foundation and the manifestation is not the relation in which I take interest. I would also like to remind you that I work towards women's liberation and more generally human liberation. And this requires us to favour singularity with respect to all sorts of gregariousnesses that, in my opinion, the words ending in 'ism' presuppose.

G.H.: It seems that the cessation of your contract at the University of Vincennes was related to the content of your second doctorate *Speculum*. Do you think that feminists still face such challenges within the Academy today?

L.I.: It is difficult for me to answer this question. I am not a feminist within the Academy. I think that the reactions are various and ambiguous. Today, women are promoted on the condition that they remain respectful of academic customs, context and traditional culture. Now, for a woman, having access to the Academy represents such an important promotion that she often forgets the necessary change of traditional culture. It is very difficult for her to realize both the gestures in the same time: entering the academic world and modifying it. Indeed, it could happen that women become more formally academic than men are, because they stay in the Academy without really sharing the culture which takes place there. Stressing formalism, then, could be their way of belonging to the Academy and of being welcomed into it. The problems begin when, in this place, a woman challenges the manner of thinking and of acting that the Academy has not, or not yet, made its own. And this was the case with *Speculum*.

G.H.: You have separated your work into three distinct stages: a critique of masculine subject identity; the problem of defining female subjectivity; and the problem of defining a relationship between two (sexed) subjects – a 'double subjectivity'. Would you say that this latter stage sets you apart from other 'philosophers of difference'?

L.I.: First, I would like to specify that the first stage is rather a criticism of Western culture as being founded by only one subject who claims to be neuter, neutral, and universal while in fact it is masculine. What I intended to construct in *Speculum* is a culture of and between two different subjects. From the beginning my work is devoted to sexuate difference. I try to promote a difference which is not the same as that present in the majority of discourses of Western thinkers and of most of us. Generally, difference is understood as quantitative and not qualitative. Of course, 'quantitativity' can assume various meanings. The difference in Hegel's work and in Marx's work refers to a relation to quantity that is not the same, even if it remains quantitative, as is generally the case in a culture of only one subject.

Man and woman are irreducible the one to the other: they cannot be substituted the one for the other, not because of a quantity – one would be better than the other, one is the first and the other the second, for example – but because of a difference in being and existing, that is to say a qualitative difference. Agreeing with this and putting it in practice constrain us to enter another logic. Without understanding this necessity, it is not possible to approach my work. In my work, the negative is endowed with another sense and function with respect to our tradition. In Hegel, for example, the negative works in order to reduce the all to the one, the One. To the contrary, I use the negative to maintain the duality of subjectivities. And this is possible, starting each time from two subjects who belong to different worlds as is the case for man and woman. The difference I implement in my thinking cannot take place between the one and the multiple, as is generally the case in Western thought. It refers to a real and concrete difference between two subjectivities, a real that can be elaborated but without abolishing the two and the difference between the two. Contrary to other philosophers of difference, I start from a real and concrete difference that is, as such, a universal which cannot be overcome without abolishing the universal itself.

G.H.: You have previously suggested that although you and Simone de Beauvoir were in agreement that women are 'the other sex,' she responded to this by refusing to be Other, whilst you embraced the difference in order to transform the relationship. How might that relationship be transformed?

L.I.: I prefer to say that woman represents the emergence of the other with respect to Western tradition. To designate such an otherness as 'the other sex' runs the risk of reducing the difference to the sex, strictly speaking, without considering the global identity. For this reason, I increasingly use the word 'sexuate difference' and not 'sexual difference.' Similarly, I do not use the word 'the Other' to refer to woman. I consider that it is important to maintain the difference between vertical transcendence and horizontal transcendence, and to keep the capital letter to designate vertical transcendence. In a way, the absolute and perfect same: the Same. My interpretation of woman as other differs from that of Simone de Beauvoir. According to her, woman is second with respect to man. Simone de Beauvoir remains in a culture of only one subject in relation to which the others are quantitatively different. My idea of otherness is more radical. The difference now is qualitative, and the negative is not used to compare two subjects: it maintains the duality of the subjects and of their worlds. This requires entering another logic, as I claim in *Speculum*. The misunderstandings about my work testify to the difficulty of accomplishing the passage from one logic to another.

G.H.: Does sexual difference act as a model for the appreciation and recognition of other differences?

L.I.: It is not a question of being a model. Sexuate difference is the most basic and the most universal difference. It is also the difference which operates, or ought to operate, each time, the connection between nature and culture for everyone. This connection is specific to girl and woman in comparison with boy and man. The feminine subject does not relate to the self, to the other(s), to the world as a masculine subject does. This does not depend only on bodily morphology and anatomy or on social stereotypes, as many people imagine. Rather, it is a question of relational identity that precisely realizes the original connection between body and culture. I am afraid that people who claim to be materialist cannot agree with the crucial role of our sexuate body in the construction of a cultural world. Now, it is not the same to make love in oneself or outside oneself, to engender in oneself or outside oneself. Neither is it the same to be born from the same gender as one's own or from another gender, and to be able to or not able to engender as one's mother did. These basic original givens determine a psychic and cultural identity peculiar to each sex, whatever could be the differences between a man and a woman.

G.H.: You have indicated that feminisms have tended to get lost in saying 'I' whereas you would prefer to make visible that the 'I' is a subject that is two (*je indice elle*); both subject and object. Can you explain what you mean by 'object' in this context?

L.I.: I do not understand your question very well. Of course, if feminisms or feminists use 'I' as is usual in our tradition, they cannot make a subject or a world emerge as different from those that men have promoted. Could such subject or world contribute towards women's liberation? In my opinion, they rather contribute towards women's repression, even though they are assumed by women themselves. It could be important here to clarify what I wrote about mimicry as a strategy and what is said about my supposed favour for mimicry. The question is: How can we leave a culture of only one subject to enter a culture of two different subjects? In some analyses, I propose to allocate to each subject a clue which indicates their sex. If this clue refers to an objectivity of the subject – who is male or female, masculine or feminine – it is not, for all that, a question of reducing the subject to an object.

G.H.: In *I Love to You*, you write that 'it's not as Simone de Beauvoir said: one is not born but rather becomes a woman (through culture) but rather that: I am born a woman, but must still become this woman that I am by nature'. Could you clarify how this is not an essentialist claim?

L.I.: For Simone de Beauvoir, becoming a woman amounts to submitting oneself to sociocultural stereotypes in relation to woman. For her, a positive becoming in the feminine does not exist, and entering a cultural world signifies adopting the culture in the masculine which, for centuries, has corresponded to our tradition. The cultivation of the self for a woman in a way implies becoming a cultivated man. The woman then becomes split into a female and a masculine belonging. Furthermore, entering our traditional culture, women share its values, including its essences. The essences remain in a culture of one subject, whatever the strategy of ambiguity – or ambivalence? – for destabilizing them, which can result in a worse nihilism.

For my part, I think it is better for a woman to cultivate herself in a feminine way; that is, to cultivate her female belonging through feminine values. Of course, this needs us to leave our past culture – of only one subject – to enter a really different culture based on the relation between two subjects not subjected to one another. In my thought and practice, the way of defining these subjects is already relational, and it takes into account, from the beginning, body and spirit or soul without separating them. The scission between female and feminine identity thus no longer exists. Moreover, the relations between the two subjects are found from their different ways of relating to the self, to the other(s), to the world. They then exclude the existence of immutable values or essences which could be shared by all people. It is all the more so since each subject, even if specific, is each time changing because of the relation(s) with another subject who does not share the same world, the same values.

G.H.: It has been said that you advocated strategic essentialism, especially in works such as *This Sex Which is Not One*. Would you agree with this, and, if so, would you still recommend it?

L.I.: I am often surprised to hear the comments concerning my work! Could it be the lack of essences which allows people to say anything and everything about my thinking? It is certainly a lack of perception with respect to the transcendental at work in it. I return to your question. From *Speculum*, I said that I intended to define a culture of two subjects, but this needed to elaborate a means to construct a culture in the feminine. *This Sex Which is Not One* belongs to both the stage of criticism in my work, the first stage, and the stage of searching for specific ways of cultivating a feminine identity. Could it be this task which is confused with essentialism by some people? It was realized in order to reach the possibility of being two.

G.H.: Michel Foucault described this century as Deleuzian and both you and Gilles Deleuze talk about 'becoming-woman' as a way to move beyond (masculine) subject-identity. Could you say how your concepts differ?

L.I.: As far as I am concerned, 'becoming woman' or 'becoming a woman' correspond to cultivating my own identity, the identity which is mine by birth. For Deleuze, it amounts to becoming what he is not by birth. If I appeal to a return to nature, to the body – that is, to values that our Western culture has scorned – Deleuze acts in the opposite way: according to him it would be possible and suitable to become someone or something which is without relation with my original and material belonging. How could this be possible above all from the part of a man with respect to becoming woman? Putting on the stereotypes concerning femininity? Deleuze would want to become the woman who Simone de Beauvoir did not want to become? It would be amusing to present a dialogue between the masculine identity of Simone de Beauvoir and the feminine identity of Deleuze! Of course, I can imagine why Deleuze wanted to become a woman, but also an animal, to shake his traditional masculine identity. But I would like to stress that he adopted such an idea at the successful time of women's liberation. I thus have some doubts about the intention of such a becoming feminine. Could it not happen to appropriate the success that women were gaining? Is it not then the same gesture as men made during our whole tradition? Why, in this time, have some distinguished thinkers suddenly wished for becoming women or feminists instead of trying to reach a neither neutral nor universal but masculine identity? The least one could say is that they have created a great confusion in relation to a budding culture in the feminine. It was not really respectful of the efforts of women to liberate themselves from the subjection to a culture in the masculine!

G.H.: In your influential essay 'Divine Women' (cf. *Sexes and Genealogies*) inspired by Feuerbach's *The Essence of Christianity*, you argue that 'as long as woman lacks a divine made in her image she cannot establish her subjectivity'. Is it possible or even desirable to understand God as a way to reflect the ideals of female or male subjects?

L.I.: In many traditions the divinities are sexuate, as humans are, and they offer help to human becoming at the different stages of its journey. Monotheism intends to enter another era. But if monotheism represents an accomplishment of humanity, it can quietly tolerate the other stages of the journey towards the divine. I am afraid that many people pretend to reach monotheism without having covered the other stages towards deification. They then contrast the radical otherness of God with the otherness of the other, in particular the sexuate other; that is, vertical transcendence with horizontal transcendence. I could agree with difficulty with such an alternative, which precisely has been used to subject woman to man. It is also important to notice that God, amongst other masculine attributes, is called 'the Father', thus is sexuated even in monotheism – as is the Trinity. Could it happen that women project onto God the otherness that they feel with respect to man because she cannot recognize him as radically other, and he cannot maintain his status of other?

G.H.: In works such as *I Love to You*, you call for the 'spiritualization of bodies'. Could you clarify what this means and how it connects to your idea about the 'sensible transcendental'?

L.I.: Instead of the repression of spirit on body, which is usual in our tradition, I prefer the transformation of body as living matter into spiritual matter. There exist some phenomena in our religious culture that can evoke what I am trying to say, for example the transfiguration of Christ. But they are quoted as exceptional phenomena and not as a normal way of spiritualization. Eastern cultures have disclosed to me this other path. There is no longer a question of dividing spirit and body, the one having to lay down the law on the other, but of transforming a vital energy into a spiritual energy at the service of breathing, of loving, of listening, of speaking, and of thinking. Such a process transforms, one could say transmutes or transfigures, little by little, our original bodily matter into spiritualized bodily matter, as I explained notably in *Between East and West*.

I consider such a spiritual journey as being more adult and also more religious. The division into body and spirit results from a philosophical Western logic which is not especially religious. Transforming or transmuting the matter, keeping it as matter, makes possible the existence of a sensible transcendental, whereas the split between body and spirit renders it impossible because the transcendental then corresponds to a removal from sensibility.

G.H.: How do you think a feminist vision of God could help us to move beyond religious fundamentalism – Islamic, Christian, Judaic – and find peace?

L.I.: I think that to move beyond religious fundamentalisms is necessary; that is, a culture of two different subjects is necessary, that is a culture in which we have to coexist in difference and to accept that our own values are not the sole and unique values. The worse conflicts happen between those who are the same and confront each other about their values, each one claiming to have reached the top. Thus inside all the 'ism' systems or groups – including feminism, which moreover and fortunately is not one – and between all the 'ism' systems of groups, peace remains unlikely. Contrary to what many people think, sameness, equality, identity, etc. do not prepare for peace but for conflicts, because people then remain in a quantitative viewpoint. Difference – of course not hierarchical, thus quantitative, difference – is more able to pave the way towards peace. It could also allow us to avoid fundamentalisms, keeping the horizon of truth open, including of the religious truth. Difference, as I try to practice and promote, is also a means of each time respecting the otherness of the other, a thing that prepares for peace and coexistence with everyone. In fact, it is an excellent regulator for keeping democratic behaviour.

G.H.: How might you respond to the concern that your emphasis on 'sexual difference' as the key with which to unlock 'differences' simplifies the complexity of our contemporary political world, underplaying, for example, questions of race, sexuality and culture?

L.I.: My way of approaching sexual and sexuate difference is really difficult to understand and put in practice because it is different from that which is usual in our tradition. It requires us to change our habits of thinking and of acting. Many people who take an interest in it grasp only certain elements without considering the foundation of such a thought. This brings about many misunderstandings, even amongst people who claim to share such a prospect. One of these consists in contrasting my way of conceiving thought and practice concerning sexuate difference with that of treating other differences: of race, of culture, of generation, etc. I know that it is fashionable today to divide the problem of sexuate difference and the problem of difference of race, of culture, of generation, etc. and to affirm that the first concerns intimate life and the second the political world. I cannot agree with this separation, as I explain in *Democracy Begins between Two* and 'The path towards the other' in *Beckett after Beckett*. I am afraid that this opposition contributes to the reduction of attention and efforts to change our customs and habits relative to sexual and sexuate difference. Now our behaviour with respect to difference of races, of cultures, of generation, etc. often results from a lack of cultivation of our sexual instincts, our most basic instincts in relating with the other(s). Another thing: the cultures and traditions are, in great part, constructed starting from sexual and sexuate difference, at the level of genealogies or marriages and alliances. How could it be possible to distinguish a culture with respect to our own without taking into account the different way of dealing with sexes or genders in this culture? And, for example: Are not the problems about the Islamic veil sexual or sexuate problems? And could not the separation of private and public life contribute to the subjection of women, as women working towards their liberation in the 1960s and 1970s claimed?

G.H.: In your view, what are the greatest challenges facing us today?

L.I.: The greatest challenge which confronts us today concerns the evolution of humanity as such. In my opinion, the matter is no longer one of proving our capability of mastering the world – be it the moon or the most minute particle – but of questioning about what or who is a human being and of seeking to reach, become and accomplish our humanity. Humans have searched for these outside themselves through dominating the world and constructing worlds of their own. The time has arrived for turning in ourselves and undertaking an inner journey. For such a task, we precisely have to leave the 'facing us' which has determined our logic of representation and our discourses or acts. I think that recognizing the other as other and seeking to meet and coexist with respect for our difference(s) could be our guide for reaching another stage of our becoming humans.

Bibliography

Howie, Gillian, with Stace Gillis and Rebecca Munford (eds), *Third Wave Feminism* (expanded 2nd edn; Basingstoke: Palgrave Macmillan, 2007).

Irigaray, Luce, *Speculum: Of the Other Woman* (trans. by Gillian Gill; Ithaca, NY: Cornell University Press, 1985).

—— *This Sex Which Is Not One* (trans. by Catherine Porter with Carolyn Burke; Ithaca, NY: Cornell University Press, 1985).

—— 'Divine Women', in *Sexes and Genealogies* (trans. by Gillian C. Gill; New York: Columbia University Press, 1993), pp. 55–72.

—— *I Love to You: Sketch for a Felicity Within History* (trans. by Alison Martin; London and New York: Routledge 1996).

—— *Democracy Begins Between Two* (trans. from the Italian by Kirsteen Anderson; New York: Routledge, 2000).

—— *Between East and West: From Singularity to Community* (trans. by Stephen Pluháček; New York: Columbia University Press, 2001).

—— 'The Path Towards the Other', in *Beckett after Beckett* (eds Stan Gontarski and Anthony Uhlmann; University Press of Florida, 2006), pp. 39–51.

—— *Luce Irigaray: Teaching* (London and New York: Continuum, forthcoming 2008).

A Feminine Figure in Christian Tradition

Conversation between

Luce Irigaray, Margaret R. Miles and Laine M. Harrington

Margaret R. Miles and Laine M. Harrington: As scholars in historical theology and the philosophy of religion, we would like to thank you for this opportunity for dialogue. More importantly, we would like to thank you for your work, which holds a distinct relationship to the Western notion of 'discourse' and potentially impacts upon the discourses of numerous fields, including religious studies. Indeed, your work is particularly inviting to many in religious studies. In part, this may be because of the discipline's long-standing relationship with the majuscule *Logos*, or Christianity's 'Word' of God, which are influenced by the philosophical *logos*. But, in part, many in our field appreciate the 'spiritual' nature of your work (its openness, its ability to breathe, its sense of otherness), often reminiscent of our best intentions for any discourse about 'God'.

It is an honour, then, to converse with you on the themes of your article 'La rédemption des femmes' (the redemption of women). Your article, a personal struggle to critically appropriate the meaning of the Incarnation from a Roman Catholic perspective, offers several insights we would like to pursue a bit further with you.

In 'La rédemption des femmes', you present the doctrine of the Incarnation as a challenge to move towards 'a more accomplished feminine identity' ('La rédemption des femmes', in *Le souffle des femmes*, p.186; the English version was not available when we began to conduct this conversation: 'The redemption of women', in *Key Writings*, p. 151). But this cannot be accomplished in isolation. Since men and women relate differently to the world, both are needed if the whole world is to be redeemed. You suggest the image of the Virgin and Child as one such redemptive couple. To achieve such redemption, the problem of male and female self-actualization (becoming) must be transposed from the natural (physical) to the spiritual. You suggest that Mary's virginity was most importantly a spiritual virginity by which she maintained an active inner integrity. It would seem, then, that a woman's becoming has two steps. She must first develop a strong subjectivity. Following this, she would find herself capable of taking responsibility for the needy public world. If we have understood you correctly, you suggest that religious symbols can be valuable in aiding woman's quest for both the integrity and liberation of herself and others.

In particular, your use of the Virgin Mary as a powerful Christian symbol intrigues us. Certainly, many scholars acknowledge Mary's potential for valorizing women. But, numerous others point to the use of her as an intended move towards inclusion that falls short. In other words, since Christian theology has authored much of Western patriarchal culture, 'woman' is represented (i.e., excluded) in Christianity in similar ways that she has been (dismissed) in Western culture.

Many (male) theologians will disagree with this, saying that women have always been welcome to practice the faith, but feminist theologians point out that women have not been permitted to have interpretive or leadership roles. Hence, women's responses to such an exclusionary culture generally follow three routes: (1) they leave the church and their tradition entirely; (2) they remain within their tradition, attempting to change what they can; or (3) they begin a completely new tradition. Oftentimes, this third option entails a retrieval of what is referred to as the 'Goddess tradition' with its worship of the feminine. It appears to us that your reading of the Incarnation, which incorporates Mary, falls somewhere between the second and third options. In other words, you appear to suggest that we remain within the tradition by attempting a new (hence, feminine or spiritual) interpretation of Mary's virginity.

With this said, we would like to begin by taking a few steps backward, by alluding to questions of why one chooses to remain within the Christian tradition, with its marginalization of women and their exclusion from leadership roles. You have suggested that you choose to remain because it is *your* tradition ('La rédemption des femmes', p. 185; 'The redemption of women', p. 150). But, as we write, we wonder, is personal history or identity with a particular tradition enough? We would like to pursue this notion by investigating with you the following: Mary in Relationship, Mary and Language, and Mary and the Politics of Interpretation.

Luce Irigaray: Before trying to answer your questions that I received in writing, I would like to make some comments about your introduction and the questions themselves.

I had difficulties realizing this work. You talk about a 'conversation' but, at least at first, I could not feel your presence and I asked myself what could be your own necessities when putting such questions. It was not clear to me that you were trying to make your way towards a feminine spiritual embodiment. Your questions appeared to me to stop at a mental level and above all to relate to debates with persons external to our conversation. I did not know how I could situate myself and talk to you. This is the reason why I took such a long time to answer you.

As I repeated a few times in my texts: it is necessary to start again from past events, figures and words to liberate their potentialities from restrictive, partial, indeed erroneous interpretations. If so many people have been faithful to certain values, it is because they convey realities to consider, or rethink, before simply relinquishing them. Having an external standpoint with respect to our tradition is useful for accomplishing a gesture of interpretation of it. At the beginning of the text to which your questions refer, I wrote that after having abandoned my tradition for many years, I returned to it in order to question it and not to blindly submit to it. I added that this gesture is useful for myself but is also useful for all women and men in search of their own liberation. This possibility of a questioning return resulted, amongst others, from practicing yoga and approaching other traditions, which compelled me to understand better, and without blind submission, my own tradition and values. The interest in other traditions and religious figures or divinities allows me to freely question those of my own story and education and to realize some intercultural comparisons. It is the case with Mary, even in relation to incarnation, and other feminine religious figures that exist in traditions less patriarchal than ours and it would have been suitable to keep and maintain free from patriarchal investments.

A last word, before answering your questions. If I understood you properly, you belong to a Christian tradition. But your use of the word 'symbol(s)' appears to take place in a Protestant interpretation of Christianity. As I received a Catholic education and lived in a Catholic context,

I am more attentive to the historical aspects, and also the personal signification of realities that you interpret as collective and atemporal symbols valid for all people. Given your own formation, it was also a surprise for me that you centered our conversation on the figure of Mary rather than on other questions treated in the same text.

I think it was necessary to make these points clear in order to make our conversation understandable for the readers, and even to have the possibility of pursuing it.

* * *

MARGARET R. MILES and LAINE M. HARRINGTON: Our four first questions are about 'Mary in Relationship'. In your article, you present the notion of the couple, suggesting that if the first couple of 'Genesis' failed; we might consider Mary and Jesus as humanity's 'first co-redemptive couple' ('La rédemption des femmes', p. 187: our translation; 'The redemption of women', p. 151). Your presentation of the co-redemptive coupling of Jesus and Mary alludes to the complexity of your work, which prefers the horizontal to the hierarchical in relationship. But, the idea of Mary and Jesus as 'couple' still frames Mary in the (m)other role (in relation to divinity). Would you elaborate on your notion of the couple with specific regard to Mary and Jesus? Also, in some of your other work, you extend the notion of the couple. Must a couple always be male and female? Would the notion of a couple also include those whose differences affect us in other ways?

LUCE IRIGARAY: According to the Bible, the first couple created by God demonstrated its inability to live happily as a couple. Adam and Eve tried to overcome the power of their creator by becoming as him. It is through generation and not only creation that the sin could be amended; that is to say, that God the creator needed a woman in order to make amends for the original sin. It was thus necessary to have recourse to a human woman and her capability for begetting. This woman had to be a virgin. My interpretation of virginity does not allude to the mere physiological hymen but to the capacity of reaching and keeping her own integrity, notably by internalizing her own breathing. If God is presupposed to have created man and woman thanks to his breathing, the redemption of humanity could only happen through the union of divine breaths in a woman, the breathing of God uniting with Mary's virginal breathing. In the two cases, it is a question of engendering and, one could say, of a search for a way of engendering a valid couple. At this stage, the emphasis of the couple is put on genealogy and the necessity for a couple to succeed in realizing a horizontal couple, which is able to become divine. If the Old Testament tells us of the stage of creation and sin, the New Testament tells us of redemption. But it stops with the generation of a divine son. We have not yet reached the time of the divinization of the man–woman couple. I wrote in some texts that this perhaps could happen in the third time of Judaeo-Christianity, the time of Spirit. But it depends on the manner of interpreting the word Spirit.

Many times I allude to coupling because it is the privileged place of a relation between human subjects. The male and female, or rather man and woman, couple is basic for joining and maintaining a human exchange: they represent the two parts of the human species who have to enter into relation while respecting their difference, which allows them to pass from simple naturality to spirituality. It is true at all the levels of this coupling: genealogies, marriages, but also brother–sister and so on. All the kinds of couples will only succeed in respecting the two parts with difficulty if they do not respect the sexual, or better the sexuate, difference.

Another thing: putting the stress on the couple is particularly crucial for questioning our tradition which concealed the importance of the man–woman relational couple by substituting for it the logical couples of opposites.

M.M. and L.H.: You write that the tradition specifies that Mary herself was conceived without sin ('La rédemption des femmes', p. 206; 'The redemption of women', p. 162). Could you elaborate on your statement that the conception of Mary would require, then, two women (mother and daughter) in a rapport of virginity to give birth to a divine child ('La rédemption des femmes', p. 206; 'The redemption of women', p. 162)? Does such a notion suggest another sense of coupling – in this case, the forgotten divinity within mother–daughter, sister–sister or friend–friend genealogies?

L.I.: The virginity of Mary – at least as I think of it – requires that she escapes a maternal incest; that is to say, an intensely close relation to or with her mother. To keep her breathing free, Mary needs her mother to have also reached autonomy and the internalization of her breathing. Otherwise, Mary ought to separate violently from her mother and could then attain virginity with difficulty. Now this virginity is necessary to give birth to a divine child. It is certain that such a mother–daughter relation involves a spiritual dimension and not only a natural dimension. This could explain the presence of feminine divinities at the beginning of our Western tradition. Unfortunately patriarchy did not respect these divine genealogies and made the mother–daughter couple fall into a natural state again. Women who today appeal to a return to matriarchy too often forget that this gesture is not possible in our present culture without turning back to a mere naturality which cannot work towards feminine liberation.

In our tradition, representation of a divine dimension in the sister–sister or feminine friend–friend coupling seems to be lacking. These couplings look like antagonists rather than spiritual relationships. Now the sister–sister coupling is basic in matriarchal culture.

M.M. and L.H.: You speak of difference in women's and men's 'natures'. Is this notion similar to the differences that occur in the socialization of women and men? Could construing feminine–masculine difference as the result of socialization rather than 'nature' give greater hope for change? For example, many women and men work hard to develop the ability to choose values and behaviour not instilled by their socialization to femaleness/femininity or maleness/masculinity. Does your image of women and men take this into account? How does the idea of women's and men's natures affect those of 'other' sexualities? Does Judith Butler's argument that gender is performative, that is, 'an incessant and repeated action of some sort', 'constituting the identity it is purported to be', help to explain the fluidity of genders within the 'couple' that you imply? How would a focus on the community rather than the couple influence difference?

L.I.: The best chance for change is the elaboration of a culture of our natural difference(s), of the woman–man difference(s). What prevents this culture from existing is the fact that our Western culture has been elaborated by only one subject, who has blindly used his particularities in the construction of our tradition. The interpretation of this tradition makes it clear that it obeys the necessities of a masculine subject and not of two different subjects and the relation between them.

Our present socialization is based only on masculine subjectivity, which claims to be a neutral identity with two sexed polarities. Then cultural difference(s) become stereotypes which result from a lack of cultivation of our natural sexuate belonging and the submission of one subject to the other. Of course, pursuing the path of socialization as it already exists will make the situation worse. And to try 'to develop the ability to choose values and behaviour not instilled by their socialization to femaleness/femininity or maleness/masculinity' is a good intention. But how could we realize this? It would imply that these values already exist and we are capable of freely choosing them. Now it is not yet the case. Before acting in this way, we have to know something about what could be an identity of our own. Of course opposing only social stereotypes does not suffice; it implies remaining in one single past culture with its polarities.

I cannot agree with the argument that gender is merely performative. Firstly, it would be important to distinguish between sex and gender in order to understand the meaning of such a statement. Does it imply that gender is simply a socio-cultural construction? By what or whom could it be realized? If it is imposed on man and woman, it does not result from their own action: they are acted upon and not acting. In the ways in which man and woman act, it is possible to distinguish what belongs to an identity and what is induced through social stereotypes. I tried to make this clear through analyses and interpretations of discourses produced by children, adolescents, and adults (see, for example, the texts on language in *Key Writings*). We are neither pure nature nor pure culture. Sexuate belonging acts as a bridge between the two. This bridge is specific for man and woman because their relational sexed belonging is different. In Judith Butler's statement that you quoted it seems that a subject could alone determine its own identity. This partakes of the illusion that a single subject exists and not two different subjects who intervene the one on the other as different relational identities, and this at all the levels and in all the situations and decisions in which we are implicated.

Of course, we are more or less conscious of such an intertwining but an attentive, and even scientific, observation can prove that it exists. The 'fluidity of genders' could happen through such an intertwining but it can only happen and be kept when we are faithful to our own sexuate identity. I prefer to talk about fluidity in the relations between the sexes resulting from respect for our difference, which keeps our identity open and changing although being specific and faithful to a proper becoming.

Perhaps it is not necessary to oppose 'community' to 'couple' as you do. Unfortunately it is often the case in our tradition because the *polis* has been elaborated amongst individuals who were presumed neuter and who were submitted to law external to their real identity. Then community is to be formed by individuals in some way abstract, and without taking into consideration their relations in difference, except as quantitative and conflictual difference. In fact, the community ought to be composed by couples whose relations reach a pacific, harmonious and fecund order, at all levels. Then difference is real and universal, a really concrete universal.

M.M. and L.H.: You write that just as women's and men's natures are different, so 'sin' (*le péché*) is different for each because they have different temptations ('La rédemption des femmes', p. 192; 'The redemption of women', p. 154–55). Whereas the sin of men is remaining too much with themselves, the sin of women is the perpetual leaving of themselves. This suggests a lack of respect for the feminine, including feminine genealogy ('La rédemption des femmes', pp. 191–93; 'The redemption of women', pp. 153–55). Would you say more about these methodologies of 'sinning' for both women and men, including your use of the term 'sin', an often misunderstood term that engages emotional responses? Why do you move so immediately from 'sin' (*le péché*) to 'lack' (*manque*) ('La rédemption des femmes', pp. 190–92; 'The redemption of women', pp. 153–55)?

L.I.: I would like to add: 'they have different temptations' and also obligations. The fault could be in neglecting one's own duties and failing to reach accomplishment of oneself, thus lacking perfection. In our tradition, the word 'sin' is generally used instead of 'being short of perfection'. I think that to situate oneself with respect to reaching perfection is better because it is more positive, dynamic and entrusts us with the responsibility of our accomplishment. I utilized the word 'sin' in this text, given the context in which it was first published, that is by an association of Catholic women who use 'sin' rather than 'lack of perfection', even if the expression appears in the Gospels, notably with the incentive to be 'perfect, as God the Father is perfect'. But I think that the word 'sin' or 'fault' sometimes could be of use in talking about our mistakes with respect to others. You could also observe that I did not translate this text.

M.M. and L.H.: The six further questions will be focused on the relations between 'Mary and Language'. As you know, we have asked these questions based on the French version of your essay (i.e., 'La rédemption des femmes'). Consequently, we are intrigued by your uses of *logos*, *Verbe* and *parole*, all of which hold historically complex relationships to ideas concerning the role of discourse, speech, language and thought. In religious and theological studies – both of which have been driven by Western philosophy – these terms play a key role in the development of the doctrine of Incarnation. Broadly speaking, it is the doctrine of the Incarnation that links divinity and humanity via 'the Word'. This 'Word' exists in Greek, of course, as *logos*, and in French as either *Verbe* or *parole*. In your first footnote you refer to John 1:14: 'And the Word became flesh and lived among us, and we have seen his glory, the glory as of a father's only son, full of grace and truth' (NRSV). It is our understanding that French editions of the Bible may translate *logos* ('Word') as either *Verbe* or *parole*, but that *verbe* is the translation upon which most often rely. Yet, in your article, you choose a translation of John 1:14 that uses *parole*. In addition, you favour the use of *parole* in your text. Would you comment on your choice of *parole*? How does the *parole/langue* distinction within the fields of psychoanalysis, linguistics and semiotics influence your choice of terms, specifically here, *parole* over *Verbe*?

L.I.: In the French version, I chose *parole*, a translation from the Jerusalem Bible. In the English version, the choice has been made by the translator and I did not verify the various ways of translating this word into English in the Bible.

I chose the word *parole* because it expresses a present actualization of meaning of which the speaker takes charge and that he or she addresses someone. What can render the word flesh is 'speaking', not discourse or *logos* as such. Furthermore, in speaking we use breathing, and meaning can remain living word and passing on of breathing itself. Perhaps my knowledge of the distinction between enunciation and utterance influenced my choice, and the fact that, as a practitioner of psychoanalysis, I experienced the benefic power of a real *parole* compared with an already defined statement. It is also possible that my religious intentions and experience influenced this choice.

M.M. and L.H.: You are well known for using language that offers many opportunities for contemplating your own philosophical presentation. For example, as a way of 'being, staying, or becoming' a spiritual virgin, you suggest the notion of 'gathering' or 'collecting' (*recueillir*) oneself (herself), in prayer, and otherwise ('La rédemption des femmes', p. 198; 'The redemption of women', p. 157). In addition to these notions of gathering or collecting, *recueillir* includes a sense of 'sheltering', of 'taking someone in', of 'home'. When it is used reflexively (as you also do), it connotes 'meditation' ('La rédemption des femmes', p. 204; 'The redemption of women', p. 161).

The very nature of *logos* desires reduplication. Hence, qualities associated with *logos* are founded upon notions of oneness and unity. Or, to put it more succinctly, in *logos* we must consider a discourse constructed in order to further itself. Turning to the Greek, we understand that the root of *logos* (*leg-*) means 'to gather'. This 'gathering', however, suggests a gathering together of 'like things' (Kittel, *Theological Dictionary of the New Testament*). Further implied in this gathering is 'order', for when things of like nature are gathered together, not only do they find their intrinsic order, but an outward sense of order also prevails. In this way, one kind of order mirrors the other. Here, we might also consider the process of narrative. Certainly, the outward parameters that define a narrative suggest order, but so does each word within it (this one comes first, that one next, and so on), until complete.

Martin Heidegger stays close to similar reasoning as he interprets *Heraclitus's Fragment 50*. Returning to the early Greek *legein* ('to lay'), Heidegger argues that 'to lay' is 'to bring to lie' which is 'placing one thing beside the other' or 'gathering'. But, Heidegger's notion of gathering includes 'picking, gleaning . . . more than mere amassing' (Heidegger, 'Logos (Heraclitus, Fragment B 50)', p. 61). He continues, 'To gathering belongs a collecting which brings under shelter' (Heidegger, 'Logos (Heraclitus, Fragment B 50)', p. 61). For Heidegger, this sheltering corresponds to homecoming. In this way, he also argues, we are able to return to ourselves.

Would you comment on the differences between these three: the notion of 'gathering' presented us by the early Greek *legein*, Martin Heidegger's reinterpretation of 'gathering', and, here, your meaning of *recueillir*?

L.I.: I do not have the text that you quote before me. Given the context in which the text first appears, it is possible that I indicated these means of gathering or collecting oneself. In other texts, I suggest remaining quiet, only keeping silent, as a way of gathering or collecting oneself, and also to feel one's lips touching one another as the threshold between the outside and the inside. I also allude to a cultivation of breathing as a manner of gathering with and internalizing oneself.

Meditation often suggests contemplating something. I more insist on the necessity of turning back before all representations and words to find or find again one's own self. This can provide all that which we are doing with a meditative dimension.

In our culture, gathering refers to constructing a world of one's own rather than gathering oneself. It is thus not yet a question of internalization. This construction of an external gathering is needed by man to leave the maternal world. For want of elaborating an identity of his own as man, it is through objects and gathering of objects or things that he escapes an intensely close relation to and with his mother. This constructed world becomes a parallel world with respect to nature, which constitutes a sort of shelter to which man refers or in which he takes refuge to cut himself off from the maternal world, at least to try to do that. If the constructed world seems to mirror the natural world, it, on the contrary, belongs to another economy, based on the arbitrary and not on the laws of the living world. Heraclitus is at the beginning of such a construction of the world based on arbitrariness: he elaborates a *logos* starting from things of the world little by little ordered according to a certain logic. Heidegger returns to these beginnings, but he often starts from existing language, and takes shelter in language itself.

Although Heidegger tries to return to the economy of *physis*, he considers the maternal world through *logos* and not through sensory perceptions. In a way, he reduplicates the Western constructed world and the way in which it surrounds humans. He attempts to interpret and partly deconstruct our tradition, but remaining in his 'house of language', he lacks a really outside standpoint to interpret it.

When I talk about gathering or collecting oneself, or with oneself, I allude to an internalized world, a positive withdrawal within the self, the home, rather than to a construction of an external world made from things, from words or from representations.

M.M. and L.H.: Another example of your textual presentation exists in your recognition of Mary as she who 'brings to the world a divine infant' (*met au monde un enfant divin*) ('La rédemption des femmes', p. 188: our translation; 'The redemption of women', p. 151). Turning away from biological (and towards spiritual) virginity, you argue that Mary accomplishes such a task through a 'proper spiritual interiority' rather than preservation of her 'physiological hymen' ('La rédemption des femmes', p. 188; 'The redemption of women', p. 152).

Clearly, your use of *l'enfantement* ('childbirth') goes beyond the notion of giving birth to a biological body, and includes the more expansive sense of giving birth to something, of bringing something into the world. In this sense, your own articulations concerning Mary's *l'enfantement* appear precisely between body and speech. Similarly, although *mettre au monde un enfant divin* means 'to bring into the world a divine child', it also holds the potential for the more expansive reading. In this way, it might be interesting to consider alternate meanings of *mettre* (generally, to 'put, place, set') in the context of your work. For example, *mettre une signature* suggests placing a signature on something, and a turn to, in this case, writing. It appears that you move towards such a reading when you write, 'To put (*mettre*) me in the quest of *my* speech (*parole*) seems the first faithfulness to a theology of incarnation' ('La rédemption des femmes', p. 186: our translation; 'The redemption of women', p. 151). Would you comment on the necessity of taking care with regard to speech? As we move from interpretations of biological to spiritual virginity, how can we become more conscious about the relationship between body and speech? Between both (body/speech) and divinity?

L.I.: Perhaps it would be fitting to turn back to a word such as 'soul' which alludes to breathing rather than to speech. This way of referring to spirituality, to the nature of spirituality in ourselves, is closer to feminine traditions which have been recovered little by little by patriarchal traditions which put the stress on language rather than on breathing. Emphasizing breathing instead of wording can also render to engendering its spiritual dimension and it could explain what is a virginity which does not amount to keeping a physiological hymen. If a woman is capable of virginity in the sense that I give to the word, she is capable of keeping an autonomous and free breathing, a breathing which serves not only survival, but to be and become a human, which always includes a spiritual dimension. This autonomy and respect for herself allows a woman to respect the breathing of the child with whom she is pregnant, not only as a condition of its life but of its spiritual existence and becoming. 'To bring into the world a divine child' could signify to bring into the world a child animated by a divine breathing.

It is of particular importance then to talk about giving birth to a someone (and not a something), or bringing someone (and not something) into the world; that is to say, not a mere body but a human already endowed with a spiritual life, with an autonomous and innocent soul. Innocence is possible because of the differentiation which exists with respect to genealogical ascendance, thus purity with respect to any sin committed by one's ancestry. In this sense, the first faithfulness to a theology of incarnation could be to keep one's breath autonomous and innocent, and to pronounce words inspired by such a breath. What this presupposes is that we cultivate breathing and do not use it only for our survival. The question, now, is: how can we be capable of a living and breathing speech, a speech which cultivates breathing and communicates with the other(s) keeping breathing alive, free, fecund in a way, always more subtle. The relationship between body, speech and divinity could take place through safeguarding and cultivating breathing. Breathing allows us to preserve a space of liberty in order to decide about our words, a space of silence starting from which we can choose, pronounce and address them. The redemption would be a new beginning of human journey thanks to a breathing, not only natural but spiritual.

M.M. and L.H.: You address the tradition's belief in the immutability of Jesus, descended from the Word of God (*du Verbe du Dieu-Père*) through the body of Mary ('La rédemption des femmes', pp. 185–86; 'The redemption of women', pp. 150–51). Here, our questions are two-fold: initially about Mary as messenger, secondly about the immutability of Jesus.

Breaking with theological tradition, you present women as the potential messengers who would faithfully (yet, firmly) welcome in a new era that safeguards women's identity, allowing them to become spiritual – 'within ourselves, as well as in and with the other' ('La rédemption des femmes', p. 208; 'The redemption of women', p. 163). Certainly, your use of 'messenger' for woman's new role refers to her ability to engender and speak difference. But, what would you say to those who continue to read 'messenger' as one who delivers a message but does not write it? How is (or is not) Mary (i.e., woman) the vehicle, conduit, vessel for the love of M/man?

While the doctrine of the incarnation specifies Jesus' human nature, theologians often perceive his (male) divinity as immutable. How do you think woman's (or, here, Mary's) new spiritual virginity will meet with the long-standing notion of the unchangeability of Jesus as divine (hence, favoured) Son? What would their conversation be like? Is it necessary to discard completely the notions of immutability, unity and oneness (i.e., *logos*) when attempting to discern new models of dialogue? Does 'dialogue' exist as part of each (masculine and feminine) discourse, or do we find it only 'between'?

L.I.: I am not sure that women already can speak differently, at least in words as they are used in our tradition or others. But it is true that in order to provide a home in herself for the different other, she has to have at her disposal a sort of language, be it only silence, which allows her to coexist with the different. At a certain level, the two living beings subsist thanks to woman. The mediation for this subsistence is first blood as providing for air.

But, being capable of this mediation without confusion between the two requires that woman cares about the internalization of breathing which gives her autonomy, one could say through a soul of her own. It is not a question here of speaking or writing as such but of gestures that intervene before speaking and writing, and that our tradition has not considered enough. A messenger can show, even keeping silent, a path or an attitude to be taken. It is in this sense that women could be messengers, able to open another era. I sometimes remind that keeping the lips touching one another, amongst others as in the sacred syllable *om*, means the safeguarding of the not yet manifested with a possible new event or advent in view. Without the capability of Mary to keep silent with respect to the *logos*, the event or advent of incarnation could not happen.

It is revealing that, on this occasion, according to the Bible, God the Father had to ask Mary for her agreement before his will could be done; that is, before the incarnation could be accomplished. Mary said 'Yes', yes to the advent of something not yet appeared, and that she was able to bring into the world. Mary is thus capable of more than the totality of that which already exists, and than the *logos* which attempts to reduplicate and order it. Attaching a too great importance to the word renders us unable to appreciate the value of Mary's gestures, including her silence.

To put the emphasis on Jesus' immutability was necessary to differentiate him from nature as such, as is the case for word itself. I would prefer that Mary's spiritual virginity could evolve according to her becoming divine. One says that a soul is unchangeable. I prefer that it evolves, becomes more subtle, for example, transforming the breathing by which it is formed in a matter more and more spiritual, divine. As far as Jesus is concerned, it is obvious that his human nature is changing. Furthermore, is it possible that his divine nature be the same before and after resurrection? Once more, I am afraid that the immutability could be a postulate obeying the same necessities as *logos* itself.

The conversation between Mary and Jesus could be focused on the simple and useful things of the daily life, or questioning about spiritual realities. But, this depends on their capacity of evolving. If Jesus' soul is presumed immutable, he could converse with this mother only with difficulty!

In my opinion, a dialogue presupposes that sense continuously evolves and always remains in elaboration through the exchanges between persons among whom no one holds the truth. It also implicates that the truth is not yet defined by external codes and constructions with respect to the two persons who are talking together.

If I understood your question properly, this sort of dialogue is at work, for example, in Platonic dialogues in which men argue about the way of reaching a truth already defined, and, according to them, immutable. I, for myself, think that a dialogue takes place between two different subjects who do not share *a priori* the same truth.

M.M. and L.H.: You suggest that if *la parole* is a vehicle of/for the divine, we must be attentive to her. In this way, she will remain healthy for us, will embody us ('La rédemption des femmes', pp. 194–97; 'The redemption of women', pp. 156–57). You mention prayer and praise in the context of this feminine language ('La rédemption des femmes', p. 197; 'The redemption of women', p. 157). Elsewhere you have written of the necessity for a feminine language – a meditative language of poetry and images – that expresses itself without relinquishing the strength of an argument to beauty. Others set up poetry as a feminine language in opposition to the sturdy, masculine *logos*. Would you elaborate on your notion of a feminine language? Does it exist in sensibility? In sensitivity? In the sensory? Would a conversation between two speaking a feminine language never risk encountering sameness? Might it equal divine language?

L.I.: I do not understand why you use 'her' to designate '*la parole*'. Could you explain that? Above all, I mentioned 'praise' as a way of praying in the feminine. The opposition between *logos* and poetry begins at a certain moment of our Western tradition in which *logos* as philosophy is considered higher than art. In other traditions, and still at the beginning of ours, philosophy, art and prayer were not separate from one another. I think that a thought and a prayer faithful to incarnation ought to remain poetry in order to express a total individual. Then each sex would have its logic and its poetry, and *logos* would no longer belong to masculine language and poetry to feminine language, as is generally the case within the categories of our tradition.

It is through many researches on language produced by children, adolescents and adults (for example 'Towards a sharing of language' and 'Being two outside tomorrow?' in *Key Writings*) that I could define some patterns of the feminine language. It is not only a matter of more or less sensitivity and sensuality, but of a difference of syntax through which the meaning is expressed. I invite the readers to refer to the texts quoted and their bibliographies. I once more repeat that women privilege relations between subjects, furthermore between two subjects of a different sex situated in a horizontal way, while men privilege subject–object relations, and, when they speak about relationships amongst persons, these occur amongst the same as the subject in a group context; the sentences which allude to relations between the sexes are negative if they situate themselves at a horizontal level, and sometimes positive at a vertical level, for example with the mother or a teacher, where they take place around an object.

Of course sameness happens in conversations between two feminine speakers. There exist stereotypes in feminine language which are not imposed from the outside but are the result of remaining in only one world, talking with people who belong to the same world. Then we could find the privilege of sensibility, sensitivity as a dimension, most of the time uncultivated, of a sexuate identity in which the relational aspect is more basically important.

Is it necessary to privilege equality? Why?

M.M. and L.H.: Similarly, with regard to the notion of feminine language and women's public responsibility, how would such a language assist women in the public task of seeking concrete justice (equality of wages, and so on)? Rudolph Arnheim has suggested that in the contemporary world, language can be profound and private, or public and superficial, not both. The 'dream of a common language' has, in media cultures that appropriate both language and images, receded from our grasp. Language that is invested with idiosyncratic and specialized meanings fails to communicate broadly and marginalizes the speaker. For example, in the United States, the word 'feminism' has been so thoroughly loaded with meanings given to it by the media that it cannot presently be used publicly without the risk of misunderstanding. Indeed, one of its public meanings is the extreme dislike of men, which is the opposite of what we would like to convey. Would you clarify the conundrum of how a 'feminine language' would expedite women's public responsibility?

L.I.: The first language that we have to consider here is a legal language. We need specific rights, and also duties, as women. In my opinion, women cannot take charge of public responsibility before being provided with a civil identity protected by appropriate laws. A woman cannot exercise public responsibilities in the name of a natural belonging (e.g., on this subject, see *Democracy Begins Between Two*, in particular the chapter on 'The representation of women'). Although they are not a minority, as some racial minorities, women need civil rights to escape her traditional natural status and slavery. The definition of rights in the feminine has to shift the emphasis of our legislation from property of goods to the respect of the person, furthermore as sexuate. As such, it will be inspired by patterns of feminine language.

In the struggles for women's liberation, we claimed that the private is public. And it is true that the feminine status has been established by a between-men public organization and that its evolution needs changes in public order. These changes, of course, are changes in the manner of communicating between citizens, above all of going from exchanging only amongst the same as oneself to becoming able to exchange with respect for differences.

Certainly, the language of the media often caricatures realities because of a lack of information and the wish to provoke some scandal. But it is difficult to deny that at least some feminists dislike men. I could quote many examples of this, notably from personal experiences. Many women who appreciated the part of my work which criticizes masculine culture, reject the part in which I try to construct a culture of two subjects, masculine and feminine. Another example: in Italy, the words 'Thought of the difference', which is a fitting way to designate my work, have been appropriated by a group of women to refer to an understanding of this work which confines itself to women as different from men without considering women and men as different from one another. I could add that I meet with a lot of aggression because I work on relations between women and men and not only relations between women.

I have already given, here, the example of the law(s), of the language and of the images. I indicate many other ways for women to express themselves in my texts. I think that using a language of their own could help women to enter into public life rather than stopping at criticism and claims.

M.M. and L.H.: Our two last questions relate to 'Mary and the Politics of Interpretation'. As scholars in religious studies, we are familiar with both the damage that has been done to women by religious symbols and their potential for liberation. Your article advises women to actively shape and use religious symbols (the Incarnation, the Blessed Virgin Mary, etc.). However, Mary Daly's question, asked long ago in *Beyond God the Father* (p. 72), still needs to be answered: If a symbol can be used oppressively and in fact has a long history of being used in such a way, is this not an indication of some inherent deficiency in the symbol? We would add to this the observation that a symbol is essentially public, resisting any private meaning. We think, for example of Edwina Sandy's sculpture, Christa, presently displayed in the chapel at St John the Divine in New York City. The image is that of a crucified woman. On the one hand, a woman is placed in the position of utmost honour in Christianity, as she who saves the world. On the other hand, contemporary visual associations of a tortured woman are pornographic and can be found at the nearest newsstand. In a society in which women are beaten, raped and murdered daily, the suggestion that a woman's torture is salvific is repugnant and dangerous. How would you respond to these notions? Should there be a difference between public and private symbols/images? Should we as women seek to 'impose' our interpretations on public discourse by discarding and replacing male interpretations, or by articulating difference alongside them? Even more, is it possible to put into language and/or imagery any religious symbol without eclipsing the indefinable?

L.I.: I do not consider the incarnation as a symbol. It rather alludes to an event of our history about which we have texts and other traces. Interpretation and faithfulness regarding this event is incumbent on everyone.

One could say the same about the Blessed Virgin Mary as mother of a divine son, even if the interpretation of her virginity provokes questions. These are partly related to the figure of God the Father. It is possible to understand the virginal pregnancy of Mary and the role of God the Father in this conception as a stage in the attempt to overcome a relationship with the mother that is too close and experienced as only natural. God the Father was probably also compensating for a lack of certainty regarding the intervention of the father in conception. We can thus see the traditional way of reading the Incarnation in Christianity as the means to avoid incest and incestuous conflicts between father and son.

This historical passage is understandable but does not justify all the repressive aspects of the patriarchal era. Before knowing *Beyond God the Father* by Mary Daly (that I thought was published later, probably because

I read it in French translation), and already in *Speculum*, I criticized the repressive dimension of the figure of God the Father and more generally of the paternal figure in patriarchy. But it is necessary to understand their historical occurrence and to be able to invent new figures to help us in our becoming. I do not interpret the incarnation, the Blessed Virgin Mary and God the Father as non-historical symbols, even if a symbolic use of their historical occurrence can be made.

I can understand Edwina Sandy's gesture. I myself thought of entitling *Marine Lover* as *Crucified Also*. I gave up this plan for two reasons: my publisher was delighted with the idea of provoking a scandal and this was not my intention; the crucifixion does not amount to a feminine torture and in particular to the more inner torture to which I wanted to allude.

I think that women have suffered, as much as Christ, to save the world, though in a different way, and that it is just to recognize this and to thank them for this. But as far as Christ is concerned, I also stressed the fact that the more important thing in Jesus' life is not his crucifixion, which is secondary with respect to his message (see, for example, 'Epistle to the last Christians' in *Marine Lover*).

But it seems problematic to compare the tortures of crucifixion to those of women who are beaten, raped and even killed. The crucifixion was justified by the spiritual commitment of Jesus and was, at least partly, assumed by him in the name of his redemptive role. A parallel can be established only with women who would share this kind of mission. I think of a figure such as Antigone, for example.

Of course private and public supports for our spiritual becoming are not the same: a singular person does not need the same help for one's journey as a community as such.

I have already written, notably in *Je, tu, nous: Towards a Culture of Difference*, about the necessity of using public support and representation for women. It is more fruitful to propose specific support than stopping at interpretation and criticism of masculine spiritual supports. We have to make our way, letting men make their own, and finding crossroads and places where we could share with respect for one another.

The indefinable must happen after all that we can define and assume, in particular our sexuate identity, in order to really belong to a spiritual or divine nature.

M.M. and L.H.: Finally, many people who choose to leave institutionalized religion turn to practices based on models of 'spirituality' that prefer self-centring, meditation and retreat from the world. While these practices offer profound opportunities for personal growth, they often become individualized, privatized, with many articulating spirituality – as an escape from the problems of institutions, society and politics – in ways that go against your work. It is in this sense that we are interested in your notion of 'spirituality'. Would you elaborate, then, on the notion of 'spiritual' virginity? What does 'becoming spiritual' really mean? Would you agree that we need models of 'spirituality' that have less to do with privatized meditation and more to do with public grace? How does this sense of 'becoming' relate to the 'becoming' presented in other of your works? How will we know when we have 'become spiritual'?

L.I.: I think that spirituality has to be first an individual practice which, of course, can inspire social and political discussions, although remaining independent of them. The relations between personal spiritual becoming and institutionalized religion are problematic because they often favour mistaking social organization for truth itself. They can also give rise to various forms of fundamentalism by granting priority to community with respect to the individual. We have to pay particular attention to this point as far as the religious dimension is concerned. No doubt, in certain cultures, religion was above all a social link. In my opinion, this is not its function for us in our times where religious dimension has to become a process of internalization proper to each one (on this theme, see the texts on religion and spirituality in *Key Writings*). This journey can be inspired by some religious value or other, notably taking into consideration the levels of the becoming of humanity that are incumbent to religious dimensions, the function of gathering, for example. But gathering together cannot substitute for gathering with oneself in our times without the risk of preventing necessary progress in individuation, in particular regarding the sexuate identity. This question is so decisive that it compels us to rethink the meaning of past religious duties in relation to it.

As far as I am concerned, becoming spiritual signifies a transformation of our energy from merely vital energy to a more subtle energy at the service of breathing, loving, listening speaking and thinking. This implies going from merely individual survival to the capacity of sharing with the other, and not only goods but breathing, love, words, thought. We thus find again the link with the other(s) but through a personal becoming, which otherwise runs the risk of being paralyzed. When I speak of a spiritual virginity, I allude to the capability of gathering, keeping and transforming an energy of one's own, besides the points already developed in my answers.

I am not sure that I understand to what you refer by 'public grace'. Once more I would like to stress the fact that we have today to take care not to mistake a public or political belonging for a personal spiritual path, because that can lead to fundamentalism and prevent coexistence between different cultures and traditions.

What do you mean by 'models of spirituality'? If you think of persons capable of providing us with the model of an exemplary spiritual journey and in this way awakening our spiritual energy, I agree that this can help our own path. If you think of abstract spiritual models imposed on us from the outside, I am doubtful about a positive result.

In a way, it has the same meaning. For example, the spiritual becoming would go hand in hand with becoming woman or becoming human.

This does not happen once and for all. We can feel whether we have progressed in becoming spiritual through the quality and the resources of our energy, our creative capacities, our capability of meeting and exchanging with the other(s) while remaining ourselves, our real tolerance towards difference(s), the nature of our desires, etc.

Bibliography

Butler, Judith, *Gender Trouble: Feminism and the Subversion of Identity* (New York: Routledge, Chapman & Hall, Inc., 1990).

Daly, Mary, *Beyond God the Father* (Boston: Beacon Press, 1973).

Heidegger, Martin, 'Logos (Heraclitus, Fragment B 50)', in *Vorträge und Aufsätze* (Pfullingen: Verlag Günther Neske, 1950); trans. David Farrell Krell and Frank A. Capuzzi in *Early Greek Thinking* (New York: Harper & Row, Publishers, 1984), pp. 59–78.

Irigaray, Luce, *Speculum: Of the Other Woman* (trans. Gillian C. Gill; Ithaca, NY: Cornell University Press, 1985).

—— *Marine Lover: Of Friedrich Nietzsche* (trans. Gillian C. Gill; New York: Columbia University Press, 1991).

—— *Je, tu, nous: Towards a Culture of Difference* (trans. Alison Martin; London and New York: Routledge, 1993).

—— 'La rédemption des femmes', in *Le souffle des femmes: Luce Irigaray présente des crédos au féminin* (Paris: Action Catholique Générale Féminine, 1996), pp. 185–208; trans. Jennifer Wong, Jennifer Zillich with Luce Irigaray as 'The Redemption of Women', in *Key Writings* (London and New York: Continuum, 2004), pp. 150–64.

—— *Democracy Begins Between Two* (trans. Kirsteen Anderson; New York: Routledge, 2000).

—— *Key Writings*, (London and New York: Continuum, 2004).

Kittel, Gerhard (ed.), *Theological Dictionary of the New Testament* (Grand Rapids, MI: Eerdmans Publishing Co., 1967).

Metzen, Bruce M. and Roland E. Murphy, *The New Oxford Annotated Bible with the Apocryphal/Deuterocanonical Books*, New Revised Standard Version (New York: Oxford University Press, 1991).

The Invisible Interlacing Between Fleshes

Conversation between

Luce Irigaray and Helen A. Fielding

Helen A. Fielding: Luce Irigaray and I began our conversation about Maurice Merleau-Ponty when I invited her to give a key-note address at the International Merleau-Ponty Circle Conference which I organized in 2003. Although it was not possible to arrange for the address, our correspondence initiated another invitation: I soon travelled to Paris to interview Luce Irigaray and our discussion quickly turned to questions I had with regard to her reading of Merleau-Ponty, as well as her ideas on art. Since I both write on her ideas and teach her work, these questions came out of a serious engagement with her thinking. On her part, Luce Irigaray pursued her reflections on the work of Merleau-Ponty as shown by an article published in an Italian journal, 'Dipingere l'invisibile'. The next step then was for me to translate this article from a French version into English. Translating can be a pleasant co-journeying, and we spent some lovely afternoons together talking about Luce Irigaray's work, Merleau-Ponty, and the use of prepositions. Luce Irigaray suggested we hold a dialogue to accompany the translation. The interview provided here is a longer version of the original (cf. 'To paint the invisible') and includes three additional questions.

Luce Irigaray's article, 'To paint the invisible', that generated the first questions, specifically addresses Merleau-Ponty's last essay on art, 'Eye and mind' (in *The Primacy of Perception*). This essay is significant since it was one of the last works he wrote and seems to lay out, however densely, the culmination of much of his thinking. In her article, Luce Irigaray not only sheds new light on Merleau-Ponty's understanding of the artist's task and embodied relations, but importantly expounds her own alternative ideas on these topics already approached in 'The invisible of the flesh' (Cf. *An Ethics of Sexual Difference*). The accompanying interview both elucidates the ideas in her article, and also clarifies questions of methodology, perceptual relations, and the sharing of our world. As in the original interview, quotes from Luce Irigaray's works are provided in order to situate the questions.

* * *

HELEN A. FIELDING:

> When Maurice Merleau-Ponty asserts that painting 'evokes nothing, and notably not the tactile' ('Eye and mind', p. 166), he forgets, in my opinion, that painting is always already tactile, like seeing itself. And if painting does not necessarily evoke the tactile in a thematic manner, and as such, it necessarily evokes the tactile in the sense that seeing amounts to being touched – by light, by colours and, in a way, by the world and by the things. But surely also by the invisible light that radiates from the other, a light which attracts and inspires me unless my flesh has become so impervious to its approach that it has lost some of its qualities. ('To paint the invisible', p. 399)

In *An Ethics of Sexual Difference* you argue for the primacy of touch over vision. For example, you write: 'A landscape much vaster but never enclosed in a map, the tangible is the matter and memory for all of the sensible. Which remembers without remembering thematically? It constitutes the very flesh of all things that will be sculpted, sketched, painted, felt, and so on, out of it' (p. 164). In returning to this theme with respect to painting, what seems to be at stake for you is that Merleau-Ponty forgets the flesh that precedes vision, a flesh that is not thought, but provides the materiality that supports both vision and thought. If the painter, for Merleau-Ponty, relies solely on vision, then what is the relation of touch to vision for him, and how could a painter achieve a relation between touch and vision that would not forget the flesh?

LUCE IRIGARAY: In my opinion, Maurice Merleau-Ponty does not forget only the flesh that precedes vision but also the flesh present in vision. When I talk about the tactile in seeing itself, I try to remember that the flesh intervenes in vision. Our culture has wanted to master life, thus flesh, including through seeing. Instead of contemplating living beings and entering in communication, in communion with them, we have been willing to dominate them by naming, understanding, reducing them to their aspect or form. Such a behaviour accompanies an economy of thought which intends to control the sensible, the growing or changing of living beings. The question is not only of preserving a flesh which ought to 'provide the materiality that supports both vision and thought', but of entering another relation between flesh, vision and thought. That is to say, of reaching a fleshy or carnal seeing and thinking, a way of seeing and thinking which obeys another logic than the traditional Western logic. For Western philosophers such as Sartre or Merleau-Ponty, seeing is not a way of contemplating but of seizing, dominating and possessing, in particular the body of the other. This transforms love and amorous life into a struggle between partners who want to master and possess the other. The relation master–slave exists not only at a mental or thinking level but also at a sensible and carnal level, notably because of a certain use of vision. Merleau-Ponty explains this in his *Phenomenology of Perception*, as I comment in the text, 'The Wedding between the Body and Language' (in the *Writings*), in the books *To Be Two* and *Key Writings*. But also when Merleau-Ponty tells us about the reproduction of the mountain by the painter, he considers the view as a means of seizing and mastering, thus reproducing, more than as a sense which can be touched and moved. Now the eyes are also that and the result of the picture will be different in this case, as I write in my text, 'To paint the invisible'.

H.F.:

> The phenomenology of the flesh that Merleau-Ponty attempts is without question(s). It has no spacing or interval for the freedom of questioning between two. No other or Other to keep the world open. (*An Ethics of Sexual Difference*, p. 183)

> He lacks the space-time, the available corporeal matter thanks to which it would be possible for him to perceive the other as other in the present, including what, in this other, will remain invisible to him. ('To paint the invisible', p. 398)

If Merleau-Ponty had been able to acknowledge sexual difference, that is, another world, another space-time, another corporeal matter, could we imagine in 'Eye and mind' the space for an interval that would allow for questioning and reflection upon experiences of perception, a questioning that would allow for the modulation of relations with the other?

L.I.: You speak about 'acknowledge'. I do not know the exact meaning that you give to the word. I would thus like to suggest that an only mental recognition does not suffice. You know that, for centuries, the understanding of sexual difference has amounted to the hierarchical bipolarity of a presumed unique subject, in which woman had a part as matter–nature–mother and man as spirit–worker–player. No doubt it is not such a conception of sexual difference which could grant to Maurice Merleau-Ponty other spaces 'for questioning and reflecting on his experiences of perception'. Rather it is a recognition, but also a practice, concerning the existence of two different subjectivities: masculine and feminine. This provides each subject with limits which open interval(s) both between the two subjective worlds and inside each world. Of course the nature of these intervals is not the same, even if they are not without link as they result from the existence of two different subjects. The difference between the worlds in which each subject dwells allows a perspective on one's own world for each and a possibility of questioning one's own way of living, also at the level of perception. The existence of two subjectivities opens new spaces created by their difference. They are not void nor filled with visible things. They are animated by the existence of the subjects and the relation between them. Beyond a perspective with respect to the visible, it is henceforth a question of a perspective with respect to the non-visible. This requires an economy in relating with the other starting at each time from their irreducible difference in comparison with myself.

H.F.:

> And if we see differently when we look together, as two, at the same landscape, it is not because a visible has been added; it is because we look differently when we share looking at. Thus, the chiasm does not simply exist between me who sees and me who is seen, me who touches and me who is touched – within a same world, my world, or from a same 'Being.' It is also that my gaze, whether I want it to or not, whether I perceive it or not, sees differently if I am not alone looking in the present. My perception itself is modified because it is shared with the other. ('To paint the invisible', p. 399)

It would seem that Merleau-Ponty's concept of the chiasm allows for mutual exchange while preserving difference. Yet you suggest that this is not the case. How might painting open up or provide for a sharing of vision between two who are different, and in doing so, modify perception while preserving difference?

L.I.: It seems to me that the chiasm to which Maurice Merleau-Ponty refers takes place between him and himself. It ensures the continuity between the inside and the outside of the subject. It corresponds to the link between an outward and an inward movement that exists thanks to the world taken as a medium or a sort of mediation between self and self. It would also be possible to think about the world used as a quasi-object and to compare the gesture of Maurice Merleau-Ponty to that of the little Hans of Freud playing with the bobbin to master his mother. But Maurice Merleau-Ponty appears to separate himself less from his mother, more exactly from a primitive relation with the mother, than did Hans. He has not reached, or does not want to reach the stage of the subject–object relation. He rather tries to remain in symbiosis with the world, a world which would substitute itself for a placenta. Indeed it is possible that the relation that Maurice Merleau-Ponty wants to establish with the world is more symbiotic than that which really exists between the placenta and the foetus. As it is commented in the interview with a biologist ('On the Maternal Order', in *Je, tu, nous: Towards a Culture of Difference*), the placenta takes into account both the mother and the foetus and keeps a certain balance between the necessities of the two. I am not sure that such a consideration intervenes in the thinking of Maurice Merleau-Ponty and that there exists for him a real duality of subjectivities. Rather he attempts to organize an infinite going and coming back between the world that he is and the world from which he emerges without ever agreeing with cutting the umbilical cord, or leaving a primitive symbiotic empathy. This probably explains his discourse on colour. But to answer the part of your question: 'How might painting open up or provide for a sharing of vision between two who are different, and in doing so, modify perception while preserving difference?' I think that the question rather is of reaching a relation between two, and two who are different, in order to modify our perception and allow us to share our vision.

H.F.:

> There, it is always a question of considering our senses, our perceptions to be mechanisms – in a certain sense biological or technical mechanisms – and not paths of and for the life which animates us, as it also animates the world and the others. ('To paint the invisible', p. 404)

Merleau-Ponty begins 'Eye and mind' with a critique of what he calls 'operational thinking', a kind of scientific thinking that does not take situation and embodied relations into account. Even though Merleau-Ponty's stated aim is to elaborate how artists are able to reveal our embodied and situated relations, you suggest that Merleau-Ponty's privileging of vision over other senses and metabolisms means that the body becomes somewhat mechanical. Does he, in fact, actually end up accomplishing that which he himself critiques?

L.I.: It is really difficult to leave a cultural epoch and to have a point of view on one's own time. In my opinion, only a relation with a different other could help us to emerge both from a past culture and from our own present world, because we then re-open our horizon in order to meet with someone who dwells in another world. Furthermore, I think that the relation with the other has to be animated by desire between the two to escape as much as possible the mechanical aspects of our bodily belonging. Another way could be to transform our elementary bodily energy into an energy more subtle and fluent. But I am not sure that this would be sufficient. In any case, to criticize 'scientific thinking that does not take situation and embodied relations into account' seems to remain a behaviour too mental and negative for succeeding in reaching another way of relating with our body. And it is not true that sciences 'do not take situation and embodied relations into account', but it takes these into consideration in a manner irrelevant to the economy of our flesh. When Maurice Merleau-Ponty says that the painter ought to reproduce all that the mountain gives him to see, he considers the eyes of the artist as instrument – a quasi-technical mechanism – which could realize a copy of the real. Such an ideal amounts to a scientific aim more than to a desire for a meeting with or between living being(s). Life as such never can be reproduced as it is. I would like to also insist on the fact that it is not only a question of 'Merleau-Ponty's privileging of vision over other senses and metabolisms'; the matter is of using our senses, thus our eyes, in another way. In fact, the question is of passing from an experience of our living being as body to an experience of our flesh. I think that such a passage can happen through relating with an other as other.

H.F.:

> My inner space is thus, for various reasons, modified by the things, and even more by the others, whom I encounter. It is inhabited in multiple ways, and the manner in which I look cannot be reduced to the mere perception of the visible external to me. I co-look with that which already inhabits me, outside of all representation. ('To paint the invisible', p. 403)

Do you think that Merleau-Ponty, in 'Eye and mind', still retains a subject–object dichotomy? Are you rethinking a notion of the subject that allows for the subject's interweaving, interpenetration with others and with the world? If so, is it possible to have an understanding of a 'subject' that does not necessarily entail subject–object relations?

L.I.: 'Thing' does not amount to 'object', as suggested by your question. Heidegger wrote a very enlightening text about this difference: 'The thing' (in *Poetry, Language, Thought*). He explains how 'object' has a part in the traditional Western economy of representation while a 'thing' differs from it. In the quotation to which you refer, it is a question of 'things' more than of 'objects'. And that allows me to say that: 'I co-look with that which already inhabits me, outside of all representation'. This also permits me to bring together, in some way, 'things' and 'others' who do not participate in the classic economy of representation as 'objects' and constitute my flesh without me being able to master them, as the Western subject tried to do with objects. Nevertheless the interaction between my subjectivity and the things is different from that with the other(s), who inhabit(s) another world than mine. But, in me, 'things' and 'other(s)' intertwine to form a world, my world. They compose my flesh and, when I look to the world in the present, I am looking with all that I am. My look is not, or very rarely, virginal with respect to the world to which I am looking in the present. It belongs to a depth of flesh which determines my vision. Maurice Merleau-Ponty – as most of the Western philosophers – barely takes into consideration this relational formation of my flesh which makes of my body a place of exchanges with other living beings. His manner of considering perception is both too solitary – or solipsistic – and confused with a primitive belonging to the world, which substitutes itself for the original participation in the maternal world. Hence a fluctuation between a quasi-technical perception of the world and an empathy with the world. The regulation which could result from a relation with the other as other is lacking – an other who is qualitatively and not quantitatively different from the subject as it is the case, for example, in genealogy.

H.F.:

> Is the task of the painter to reproduce the visible in order to allow it to be seen by those who are incapable of observing it or those who do not have the opportunity to perceive it? Or would it rather be to allow us to perceive, thanks to specific materials and gestures, that which language and music – to give but two examples – do not allow to be perceived? Especially of the invisible. ('To paint the invisible', p. 403)

How do you understand the task of the painter, in particular with respect to the invisible?

L.I.: I will answer above all the part of the question about the invisible as such. This one has not had a sufficient part in our culture emphasizing form(s) and representation(s). And thus the invisible has often been postponed or deferred onto a religious sphere around the invisibility of God. But the invisible takes part in our everyday relations with the world, with the other(s). For example, the air through which we relate to the world and, in some way, with the other(s), remains invisible. The void of the 'thing' which allows it to hold – as Heidegger commented – cannot be represented. And our interiority neither. The relations between us and the world, us and the other(s) are not visible. If we can perceive something of our interiority and our relations with the world or the other(s) through their expression or their effects, they remain invisible as such. How could a painter express them? I am not a painter but I think that it would be possible to suggest the invisible by a certain use of forms and colours – in particular white – and a certain use of perspective. Someone who perceives the invisible could transmit something of this perception in painting. There is space, spacing, and perspective relative to the invisible which could be expressed. Once more, this presupposes to live the body as flesh not as simple body, to overcome the split between body and spirit, matter and form(s) amongst others through a global relational behaviour with the things, with the other(s). This also implies recognizing that the other as other remains invisible for me and that the first gesture with respect to him, or her, is to accept and respect this invisibility; which then transforms my perception of the world (cf. the chapter 'To perceive the invisible in you', in *To Be Two* and 'Being-two, how many eyes have we?', in *Dialogues*). A simple criticism to the formal aspect of our tradition cannot reach such a transformation. The matter is of entering another co-belonging and co-existing with the thing(s) and with the other(s) that require another way of relating together through any sort of language.

H.F.:

> Thus claiming to perceive a living being simply with our eyes which, moreover, are mirror-eyes, and then to give it for others to see seems a little naïve. The same applies for believing that I could become a thing amongst the others, that I could transform the things into spectacles and myself into an other or an other into me through a specular power only. This implies that the imaginary has already been substituted for the real, and to some extent death for life. ('To paint the invisible', pp. 401–402)

Certainly you have rethought the Lacanian term of the imaginary substantially in your own work. The concept of the 'real' is also considered to be a psychoanalytic concept yet it would seem that you are referring to something very different here. Could you clarify your understanding of the 'real'?

L.I.: To understand the quotation without seeing the text, it is necessary to go back in the text to where I explain that 'we co-belong to the living world', that 'we exchange, indeed sometimes reverse, the roles between us'. And this happens not simply at a visual level but in a total way: for example, we exchange air – that is, life – with the plant world. Thus, 'Claiming to perceive a living being merely with our eyes which, moreover, are mirror-eyes' is really too simple and rather naïve. This amounts to ignoring the fact that sharing with our living surroundings is more complex, and that it escapes from our mastery through eyes and from its reproduction through images or words.

Such considerations explain my use of the word 'real' here. It is not a question of the real, nor the imaginary, which intervene in the work of Jacques Lacan. Rather I refer to the meaning of the word 'real' in philosophy. Real can be said of that which is not yet submitted to our logic, to the *logos* which rules our language. One could say, for example, that life as such is a real that becomes reality through a culture which often transforms life and living beings into coded behaviours, habits, customs, discourses and representations which somehow or other substitute for the living real. Our culture has privileged eyes as a means of mastery to the detriment of experiencing life itself. Converting a non-apprehendable real into a visual or a mental spectacle or representation still corresponds to Maurice Merleau-Ponty's approach which, in fact, remains inside the Western metaphysical tradition. Certainly, some allusions to colour could suggest something beyond any form or word. But the examples that he gives, even to speak about touch, are still visual. His attempt to interlace eyes and touch amounts to an endeavour to submit touch to eyes by seeking how to make touching visible. What colour could have a touching between two fleshes? Is not such a touching invisible when it happens?

Even when he talks about flesh, Maurice Merleau-Ponty converts the real of the flesh into a metaphysical reality, at least partly, because what happens in touching between two different living fleshes seems strange to his perception. But what is touch outside the overflowing contact between two fleshes? Our tradition apprehends with difficulty such a phenomenon because it escapes our eyes, even if touch itself takes part in our capacity for seeing. But Western philosophers, even phenomenologists, do not care very much about that. Maurice Merleau-Ponty himself talks about carnal love as a sort of master–slave struggle regarding the domination of the nakedness of the other through our eyes.

In fact, if you refer to the chapter 'The Intertwining – the Chiasm' in *The Visible and the Invisible* and my comment in *An Ethics of Sexual Difference*, you could observe that Maurice Merleau-Ponty's aim, conscious or not, is to interlace touch and vision in order to enclose himself in a world of his own. Flesh there is no longer what opens his world to another world, a world different from his own; flesh is what unites his world, a world supposedly unique and split between the in-itself and the for-itself, even at the sensible level. In order to support such a perspective on the world, Maurice Merleau-Ponty must attribute to things the same flesh as his own, becoming in this way a thing amongst other things, forming with them a sort of universal and anonymous flesh. As far as the other is concerned, this other is reduced to a thing or imagined as eyes which from the outside make possible or endanger the interlacing of touch and vision thanks to which the philosopher constitutes the closure of the world. Thus the reason becomes clear for which it is necessary for one lover to defeat the eyes of the other in order to not become a slave in carnal exchanges.

H.F.:

> Our body is not only set down or situated in space, placed side by side with other bodies, or other things. It is also intertwined with them and interlacing of those with it. ('To paint the invisible', p. 403)

An analysis of space and spatiality is central to Merleau-Ponty's work, and yet you suggest that he has not taken his thinking about space far enough – that he only thinks about it in terms of situation and not in terms of spacing, in terms of communication and relation. You suggest further that his interpretation of Descartes is flawed. Could you please speak further to your rethinking of space, and to Merleau-Ponty's Descartes critique?

L.I.: In your quotation, you made a little error. I hope you will forgive me for starting from this error to explain something. You quoted: 'It (our body) is also intertwined with them (other things or other bodies) and interlacing of those with it'. My text is rather 'interlacing of those within it'. Now 'interlacing with it' could easily enter Maurice Merleau-Ponty's discourse whereas 'interlacing within it' would with more difficulty because this could disturb his solitary relation to the world.

In fact, Maurice Merleau-Ponty's thinking, as is the case with some other discourses of posthegelian philosophers, tells us about the reversal upon the thinker of the world which has been constructed by our Western philosophy. This world has been constituted through presenting things, and others in some way, before oneself in order to be able to represent, denominate, and gather them in a whole. If things are in interaction through their position in *logos*, there is no longer a spatial interaction between them as living beings: through *logos*, which assigns a place to each, they are cut off the one from the other. Of course, the thinker – and everyone – will link them anew through *logos*, but inside a constructed space. The original living space no longer exists in which the limits of the place of each mixes, at any moment, with that of other living beings. The function of *logos* is to interrupt this mixing in order to construct a world at the disposal of man and the constitution of his identity.

Whatever the subject approached by Maurice Merleau-Ponty, for example, sensory perception, the Western metaphysical construction remains at work and implicates a certain conception of space and time appropriate to a subjectivity for whom the world is both one and unique. To take within oneself the interlacing of things and other bodies, it is necessary to discover another way of constituting a world of one's own. Instead of entrusting this task to *logos* as it has been defined – which presupposes a single subject, with at the very best those who are the same as this subject, and a single world – I propose to start from the existence and the relation of two different subjects, this difference being both natural and transcendental. Such a foundation of the world and of subjectivity provides us with another spatial delimitation and elaboration which allows us to be faithful to life while cultivating it. The relations between things and bodies, but also between myself and them, then acquire another status. I can keep them and meet with them in their living existence because the existence of another living subject, with his or her own world, provides life with limits without freezing it into essences. Maurice Merleau-Ponty's discourse on flesh itself is, in some way or other, flawed because he remains in the perspective of a single and unique subject confronting a unique world. All the reversals inside his thinking, and above all between him and the world, do not reach what happens in the meeting with another flesh. What Maurice Merleau-Ponty says about the carnal encounter reveals this lack of communication between two on this occasion.

If Maurice Merleau-Ponty is sometimes capable of a troubling discourse about his being similar to the world, this could be explained by the fact that he meets with the world, including the underground of the world, that he has constructed as man. He meets the world built through his *logos*, whatever could be his sensory approach to this world. The event which remains strange to him is: this is our flesh; that is, a living interlacing with the flesh of the other in which, if only for a little moment, we become two in one, which does not mean that we become an anonymous flesh. This event can happen only if we are able, before and after it, to keep the two and the space between two. We then enter into another relation to space and spatiality about which I began to elaborate in *I Love to You*, *To Be Two*, *The Way of Love* and *Sharing the World*.

H.F.: Making the known seem strange in order to bring it to appearance is a phenomenological technique. Indeed, you have used a variation of this practice as a textual strategy in your analysis of philosophical writings. And yet this technique also seems to imply a distancing of the familiar, a making it other rather than a recognition of the other in me and near me. Could you comment upon this technique of making the known strange?

L.I.: I am not sure that I exactly use such a technique. Because this would suppose that I could know the other(s) and make this other strange in order to bring him, or her, to appearance. Of course something of this methodology exists, but it is almost used in a reverse way. The matter is now to make clear that the other as other never can appear to me, if not as strangeness. The other as other is what questions the aim of our philosophy to render all understandable – except perhaps God himself. I try to make appear that the other as other never will appear to me notably because this other is a 'who' and not a 'what'.

Of course I refer to the other in a more specific way than you in your demand, in which you use the word 'other' in an anonymous and somewhat undifferentiated way. You do not consider the other as a particular someone but as an undifferentiated part of an external or internal world. You follow in that the methodology of Maurice Merleau-Ponty who asserts that he is a thing amongst things, without sufficiently distinguishing 'what' from 'who' in the constitution of the world. In fact, a 'who' never can appear to me in their otherness. But the more this other is different from the Western philosopher, the more this one will reduce the other to appearance, even ideal appearance, to integrate otherness in his logic. What I try to show in my work is the strangeness of Western philosophy itself in order to lead to our understanding of the extent of the exclusion of the other as such from our traditional logic: that is, the exclusion of the possibility of another subject living in another world.

In my analyses of philosophical writings, I consider the relation between the 'who' of the philosopher and the – at least almost – 'what' of the text. Of course I do not stop with only empirical considerations about the author, but I question the logic which governs the projection of the philosopher onto a world, a truth, an absolute. In fact my methodology with respect to familiarity and strangeness is more complex than the method to which you allude. If, the first time, it could be said that I make strange the familiar to show its otherness, the second time – no doubt this partition is above all pedagogical – I let the other be in their strangeness to respect otherness itself. This is of particular importance in regard to another 'who', but it is also critical with respect to living beings and all that remains real in relation to my discourse. Beyond the fact that such a method allows me to really respect the otherness of the other as irreducible to me or my own, it also permits us to approach, from a new perspective, the traditional debate between Being and appearance.

Bibliography

Heidegger, Martin, 'The thing', in *Poetry, Language, Thought* (trans. Albert Hofstadter; New York: Harper and Row, 1971), pp. 165–82; originally published as 'Das Ding', in *Vorträge und Aufsätze* (Pfullingen: Neske, 1954), pp. 157–75.

Irigaray, Luce, 'The Invisible of the Flesh: A Reading of Merleau-Ponty, *The Visible and the Invisible*, "The Intertwining – the Chiasm" ', in *An Ethics of Sexual Difference* (trans. Carolyn Burke and Gillian C. Gill; New York: Cornell University Press, 1993), pp. 151–84; originally published as 'L'invisible de la chair: Lecture de Merleau-Ponty *Le visible et l'invisible*, "L'entrelacs – le chiasme" ', in *Éthique de la différence sexuelle* (Paris: Minuit, 1984), pp. 143–71.

—— *Je, tu, nous: Towards a Culture of Difference* (trans. Alison Martin; London and New York: Routledge, 1993).

—— *I Love to You: Sketch for a Felicity Within History* (trans. Alison Martin; London and New York: Routledge, 1996).

—— 'Dipingere l'invisibile', *Segni e Comprensione* 44 (Dec. 2001): 10–16; 'To paint the invisible', trans. from the French by Helen Fielding, *Continental Philosophy Review* 37 (2004): 389–405.

—— *To Be Two* (trans. from the Italian by Monique M. Rhodes and Marco F. Cocito-Monoc; London: Athlone and Routledge, 2000).

—— 'Being two, how many eyes have we?', in *Dialogues: Around Her Work*, special issue of *Paragraph* 25/3 (Edinburgh University Press, 2002), pp. 143–51.

—— *The Way of Love* (trans. Heidi Bostic and Stephen Pluháček; London and New York: Continuum, 2002).

—— *Key Writings* (London and New York: Continuum, 2004).

—— *Sharing the World* (London and New York: Continuum, 2008).

Merleau-Ponty, Maurice, *Phenomenology of Perception* (trans. Collin Smith; London: Routledge and Kegan Paul, 1962); originally published as *Phénoménologie de la perception* (Paris: Gallimard, 1945).

—— 'Eye and mind', in *The Primacy of Perception* (trans. Carleton Dallery; Evanston: Northwestern University Press, 1964); originally published as *L'oeil et l'esprit* (Paris: Gallimard, 1964).

—— *The Visible and the Invisible* (trans. Alphonso Lingis; Evanston: North Western University Press, 1968); originally published as *Le visible et l'invisible* (Paris: Gallimard, 1964).

Sexuate Identities as Global Beings Questioning Western Logic

Conversation between

Luce Irigaray and Elizabeth Grosz

Elizabeth Grosz: This interview took place in writing between February and November 2006. In it we consider some of the major texts published in *Key Writings* and try to explain to Luce Irigaray's readers the power and significance of the concept of sexual difference for our understanding of subjectivity or identity, our notions of philosophy or thought more generally, and for envisioning a future with two different human beings capable of living and producing together. How are we to conceive sexual difference if the very tools of thought have denied and effaced it? How are we to live sexual difference if cultures have privileged only one type of subject? These are the central concerns of this interview, which demonstrates the depth and tenacity of sexual difference and the possibilities it contains for new forms of culture, new modes of thought, and new forms of creativity engendered between the two sexes.

* * *

ELIZABETH GROSZ: It is possible, without being too arbitrary, to divide your work into three periods or phases: the first is largely occupied with the critique of psychoanalysis and with extricating the two sexes from confused conceptions that masculinize the female subject; the second could be described as a series of interventions into the history of philosophy to remind philosophers of their unspoken debts to women, the mother and to the female body; and the third, which I believe represents your current work, is directed to finding a way, socially, politically, ethically and amorously, to connect the two sexes without reverting to the domination of the one by the other. If this is a more or less accurate description of the development of your work, I was wondering whether you could explain how your position has changed (What are the new questions and concepts you direct yourself to in the present? What do you think is no longer relevant? What needed to be reconsidered?) and what in it remains the same? In part, this question seeks out how you see the internal trajectory of your writings. What is the consistency of your work? Have there been major ruptures, or small shifts in emphasis and interest?

LUCE IRIGARAY: I do not consider the trajectory of my thought to be as you suggest. I would rather say that the first part of my work amounts to a criticism of the Western tradition as constructed by a single subjectivity, a masculine subjectivity, who has elaborated a logic and a world according to his own necessities. In the second part, I try to indicate mediations which permit a feminine subjectivity to emerge from the unique and so-called neutral Western culture, and to affirm herself as autonomous and capable of a cultivation and a culture of her own. The third part of my work is devoted to defining and rendering practicable the ways through which masculine subjectivity and feminine subjectivity could coexist, enter into relation without submitting or subjecting the one to the other, and construct a world shareable by the two with respect for their own worlds.

Of course, these three stages or aspects of my thinking intertwine and interact. For example, already in *Speculum*, I talk about the necessity of a double, and even triple, dialectics in order to allow culture to take into consideration the existence of two different subjects.

If I developed my initial plan, if I progressed on the path, my position did not change. I know that this is asserted, but it is a mistake. Perhaps some readers do not understand the passage from criticism to the more constructive aspect of my work. Or how the discourse of a single person can unfold without confining itself to repeating the same things. Or even how it is possible to go from a philosophy of a single subject to a philosophy of two subjects, and what other means are then needed.

I note two main errors in the comments that I read on my work: (1) the tendency to search for an origin of my thought outside its own foundation, for example in some spiritual father that I would not recognize as such; (2) the belief that my work is more simple, empirical and common than it is, and does not require that its original path and methods be considered in order to understand something about it.

E.G.: Your earlier writings have tended to focus on philosophers rather than novelists, political activists, artists (perhaps with the exception of Freud). Do you consider your current work on the creation of sexuate rights, a civil society that adequately recognizes each of the two sexes, and the possibilities of a love between the two sexes, part of this ongoing critique of philosophy? What is its place in the history of philosophy? Or is this new work to be understood as a new kind of writing, a form of political intervention rather than philosophy?

L.I.: My work on sexuate rights begins with *Speculum*, for example in the chapter devoted to an interpretation of Hegel's ethics in *Phenomenology of Spirit*, but not only here. In *This Sex Which is Not One*, Chapters 8 and 9 talk about the status of women in our social order. I return to the argument of sexuate rights in *Thinking the Difference*; *Je, tu, nous*; *I Love to You*; *To Be Two* and *Democracy Begins Between Two*. But this dimension is already at work in my earlier writings. And my problems with some universities, psychoanalytical schools and circles, and even, more recently, my housing problems are largely due to the fact that I was, as you say, a 'political activist' in the movements for women's liberation. Also here what is claimed about my not taking part in the political movements for women's liberation is not true. Why is it said? Because most people are either theorists or 'political activists'? But not in my case . . . I worked a lot at the political level to obtain rights for women, and my struggles for sexuate rights sometimes met with painful opposition from women themselves, notably but not only, from those who demand rights equal to those of men and not rights appropriate to women.

The question of a 'civil society' and of civil rights is not strange to the history of philosophy. Of course, I can quote Hegel's work on natural and civil rights. But it is only one example that I know particularly well. If philosophy and politics usually have no immediate relation, they cannot remain irrelevant to each other. And it can happen that their connection becomes more necessary in a certain epoch, for example when it is a question of defining, or redefining, human rights, as it is the case regarding a society or a culture of two different subjects.

E.G.: You remain committed to reconsidering sexual and love relations, to developing a different conception of sexual and love relations that does not involve the reduction of the two sexes to the one (the couple, the unitary

structure of marriage, the all). You have maintained that the relation between the two needs to be indirect so that one does not swallow up or dominate the other, so that the sexual relation remains a coming together of two fundamentally and irreducibly different subjects. What is so special about sexual relations? Why are sexual relations so central to reconsidering the ways in which society more broadly needs to change to accommodate sexual difference? How do they relate to and affect other social or civic changes? Is a new sexual ethics a condition for a new social organization?

L.I.: It is not only a question of sexual relations but of sexuate identities. In all the world, only two sexuate identities exist: of different ages, races, cultures, traditions, and so on. The different cultures largely correspond to a specific way of organizing relations between sexuate identities at both levels of genealogies and marriages or other horizontal alliances. All the socio-cultural world is elaborated starting from sexuate identities. They represent the first bridge between nature and culture that various traditions will treat in different manners. Social and civic changes must necessarily take into account sexuate identities, which more or less apparently are at the root of their construction. Democracy, in particular, needs other relations between man and woman, men and women to be established. And it is through such considerations that we could pass from a local to a global democracy. Otherwise we remain obedient to abstract, moralistic and somehow repressive integration or rejection with regard to community, unless we stop at submitting to economical power.

If we agree that sexuate identities form the fabric of our societies and culture, how could we be unconcerned about sexuate and even sexual relations? Could we deal with this question in a merely objective and cold manner? Is this separation between subjective and objective possible when the matter concerns so fundamental a dimension of our being and Being? Would this separation be desirable? And what could be the truth concerning sexuate identity outside any care about the relations between the two sexes?

Another thing: our Western culture has failed to cultivate intersubjective relations, especially between man and woman, men and women. This resulted in the reduction of women to a mere nature that men blindly exploited for their own profit. A cultivation of reciprocal desire and love between two subjects respectful of their differences seems the solution to overcome the master–slave conflict which has determined our sexuate and sexual relations over centuries.

Furthermore, our sexual drives are one of the main sources of our energy. If they are not cultivated, they become instincts of possession, domination, subjection, appropriation and so on, all kinds of instincts which have ruined the relations between us, and (between) communities themselves.

E.G.: In 'You Who Will Never Be Mine' and 'The Wedding Between Body and Language' (both republished in *Key Writings*), as well as in other texts, you discuss the idea of a new mode of recognition, beyond that marking the Hegelian dialectic of master and slave, in which the recognition of the other entails producing a profound vulnerability in oneself, even unto death. If the Hegelian conception of recognition has dominated the phenomenological tradition up to and including Jean-Paul Sartre, Simone de Beauvoir and Maurice Merleau-Ponty, even as it tries to move beyond the dialectic, what would this other mode of recognition look like? What is the mode of recognition that links two fundamentally different types of sexuate being? Can there be difference without negation? Can there be a dialectic without synthesis? To what extent is this new model of recognition indebted to Hegel and to phenomenology, and to what extent does it move beyond them?

L.I.: As I try to explain in some texts – among others those that you quote, but also in the 'Preface' to *Key Writings* and the 'Introduction' to the part devoted to philosophy – the use of the negative in my work differs from that of Hegel. I use the negative to maintain the existence of two different subjects and of their worlds, while Hegel uses the negative to reduce the all, in particular every duality, to a one – One. My use of the negative serves to maintain irreducibility of the *you* with respect to the *I*, that is, the insuperable and unknowable existence, being and truth of the other. While Hegel somehow attempts to reduce the all to the same, I stress the necessity of recognizing the existence of the unknowable, the inappropriable objectivity and subjectivity that the other represents. The existence of two irreducible subjectivities, which are determined by their belonging to a sexuate identity, implies that a more total human real has to be taken into account and that the relations between real and language, life and consciousness become dependent on a triple dialectical process: one for each subject and one for the relation between the two.

At a certain level, no doubt it is respect. I could also evoke sensory perceptions, sensible and sensuous feeling and desire, consideration for irreducible otherness as a dimension of our humanity as such, interaction between two different worlds and co-creation thanks to difference, longing for transcendence between humans, wish for a cultivation and a meeting of our total beings, care about a local and global democracy, search of intercultural exchanges and of course taste for truth and so on.

Difference exists in nature itself. The question is: how can we behave with difference and define a language which allows us to meet each other and communicate taking into account our difference(s)? If negation was of use for man to differ from his maternal origin, we have now to discover the perception of the limits which exist between us: man and woman, men and women.

In a way we have to apply the negative to our own desire for the absolute in order to respect the existence and the desire of the other. At least our wish for the absolute has to evolve. Perhaps I could say that it has to give up spreading towards an infinite of our own to reach another nature. This requires us to gain a more complete autonomy and be capable of cultivating and transforming our energy. Transforming our total being – and Being – does not correspond to a process of our Western reason. It tries to lead the real to an ideal status and permanence instead of caring about transforming the real itself until its nature has become changed. Such a process requires effort and limitation from us. But it is the condition for respecting the other as other, without integrating this other into our own world and limiting the use of the negative only to earlier stages or states of our own self or world.

There will exist a synthesis in each one. A return to one's own self and a perception of the totality of the self is necessary in order to meet the other as other. This synthesis cannot be definitive; it must evolve according to the relations to one's self, to the other, to the world. A synthesis achieved once and for all as a permanent one – One – no longer exists. Although each one has to be in search of an absolute of one's own, one also has to remain able to question and put this absolute on hold in order for a meeting with the other as other to be possible.

A sort of synthesis can sometimes happen during a meeting in which, for a moment, the two worlds form a single world. But it is necessary that each one return in oneself, in one's own world, to permit such an event to happen again and a third world to be created by the two with respect for the singularity of each one. Such a synthesis seems to be really different from that of Hegel, who refers to a single subjectivity and objectivity.

Furthermore, it is now a question of a synthesis created by two total beings and Beings, and not by a consciousness which attempts to realize the final synthesis of subjectivity and objectivity belonging to one and the same real.

No doubt, Hegel and some other phenomenologists whom I quote and on whom I make comments, taught me how to reason and argue in a philosophical way. They also helped me to know the history of Western philosophy and to question it. What is absolutely strange to them is the possibility of imagining and establishing a philosophy of two different subjects. This foundation of my thought has required me to question Western discourse as sexuate, thus partial, and search for another logic and discourse, which recognize the existence of two different subjects and allows coexistence and communication between them to exist. I particularly had to question the status of representation which acts as a basic key in our Western tradition.

E.G.: To continue our interrogation of phenomenology: is it because the other is recognized as a version of myself, a being who shares with me a common humanity and who does not differ in significant ways from me, that sexual relations are understood, within phenomenology, as forms of conquest? In conquering the other's transcendence through an intimate encounter, I come to understand and attain my own transcendence. You have insisted on an 'irreducible invisible' (*Key Writings*, p. 15) in the other which is beyond vision and touch, which locates transcendence, and the interlocking of marriage, of language and body which marks my distance from and outsideness to the other. Clearly you believe that there can be a relation between the self and other which need not involve conquest, the reduction of the transcendent to the body, and a recognition of only oneself and not the other. Can this be thought within phenomenology? Or do we need other philosophical frameworks? What would these be? What discourses and concepts might help us develop an understanding of the intersubjective?

L.I.: It is not only a question of sexual relations strictly speaking, but of all relations. You could recall the master–slave relation that, somehow or other, takes place in all our relations and will subsist as long as we do not leave our logic for another. I could say, a quantitative logic for a qualitative logic, but this needs to be developed as I have done and continue to do in my work. Most people, all the time and at all levels, act as conquerors. Certain phenomenologists, renowned for their ethics, have described sexual relations as a form of conquest, but this could be generalized to almost all human behaviours. Until we realize that we have to modify our relation to transcendence and we really accomplish that, we will continue to immolate the other, others, the world and in a way ourselves to a longing for a transcendence outside of our human capabilities and fundamental duties.

I talk of an irreducible invisible in the other as corresponding to the centre, the nucleus, the core of the organization of his or her being or Being. This centre, nucleus or core remains invisible as such, and we can perceive something of it only indirectly through decisions, gestures or words, and also modifications of the body itself. This core of the subjectivity of the other, must remain a mystery that transcends me. Even if this other has not yet reached a proper relation to transcendence, I must respect his or her irreducible otherness. I think that a relation to and with the other as such requires us to give up all the conquests which amount to abolishing the duality of the subjects.

In my own thought, subjectivity, body and transcendence cannot be separated, particularly when it is a question of relations between two different subjects. If the subjectivity of each one does not secure a bridge between nature and culture, relations in difference cannot happen.

In my opinion, a 'recognition of only oneself and not the other' is meaningless. There is always some other – or Other – who influences my recognition of my own self. This other – or Other – is more or less conscious, more or less mediatized by a socio-cultural context, he or she is more or less situated in the same time and at the same level as mine, but this other exists. And it is precisely this other who acts on my recognition of my own self, and who in part allows me to recognize the other here and now present to me or prevents this recognition.

It seems to me that I use a phenomenological method, at least in part, to approach the question of the other. Of course, phenomenology itself needs to evolve when it takes into consideration domains that it had not yet approached. And I have recourse to methods that phenomenologists did not or do not yet use. For example: I use dialectics in a different way, notably at the service of relations between different subjectivities; I have recourse to perception in a manner more embodied, sensitive and sensuous, and above all more relational; I stress a necessary structuration and cultivation of our global being and Being; I recognize an insuperable difference between us and our worlds; I suggest that the transcendental has to remain also sensible in order to act between us as horizontally transcendent one to the other; I practice analysis of discourse as a quite crucial method to open up to intersubjective perspective and behaviour; I stress both opening to the other and returning to and in oneself in order to preserve the duality of subjectivities; I make clear the importance of silence to keep an availability capable of welcoming the other as other; I allude to an essential culture of breathing for reaching our autonomy and cultivating our life towards its sharing; I insist on the need for a po(i)etic dimension of language to allow us to come into presence and communication in difference, and so on.

Some of these methods can enter the phenomenological framework provided that phenomenology take into consideration some dimensions of our being and Being, in particular their relational aspects and their impacts. Unfortunately, cultivation of breathing and of energy does not yet have a share in our Western culture, especially in our philosophical tradition.

I am not sure that it is still a question of concepts. Concepts, like essences, make subjectivity dependent on a single definite objectivity. They do not permit meeting and entering into dialogue between two subjects who belong to two different worlds.

E.G.: This question of the limits of phenomenology leads to a series of new questions that have elaborated themselves only in recent political and social life. In 'Approaching the Other as Other' you make it clear that never has society addressed the question of the other more than it does in the present (*Key Writings*, p. 24). With the dramatic increase in migration and the push towards globalization, the other considered as ethnically, racially or religiously different requires more and more of a place in our understanding of ourselves and our culture although our conceptual and personal resources for understanding this other are more and more inadequate. Is sexual difference an adequate model for developing an understanding of these other differences? Why is sexual difference 'the foundation of alterity' (*Key Writings*, p. 26)? What of the racially and ethnically different other is still left over or unexplained through sexual difference? Does sexual difference have an ontological status that other differences do not? Is it at the 'origin' of other differences, as you seem to suggest: 'It is often the manner of treating this [sexual] difference . . . that is at the origin of differences between traditions, between cultures, manifesting themselves notably in customary law' (*Key Writings*, p. 26).

L.I.: The insistent question of the other does not only result today from immigrations and globalization, even if such events force us to deal with it as a matter of urgency. Since the nineteenth century, the question of the other has become an important one in our Western culture, but as a question relative to otherness within a single and unique world: the question of the other as child or as mad, for example. It was not yet a question of the other as other, that is, as a subject really different from mine, but of the other within a culture based upon a single model of subjectivity. The other was the one who was more or less true to this model.

The question of the other as other arises in our tradition with the claim of women to exist as women, that is, as autonomous subjects, set free from masculine guardianship and authority. Such a claim can end in a mere egalitarianism, but this outcome does not take into consideration women in their total and specific being and does not provide them with a real liberation as women. As it was asserted in the course of the 1960s: women's subjection comes from difference and has to find its resolution in difference. No doubt, the point is not to remain within a culture of difference which is responsible for feminine subjection, but to enter another culture in which two subjects can exist without being subjected the one to the other.

To go from a conception of sexuate difference within a culture of a single and the same subject to a conception of sexuate difference in a culture in which two subjects belonging to two different worlds can be recognized as such and coexist gives access to a new foundation of alterity. The other is no longer a sort of object towards which I at best practice tolerance, hospitality, moral or religious duties and so on. The other now represents another world with a specific organization and truth with whom I have to come to terms to be faithful to humanity.

Sexuate difference can serve as foundation of such a conception of alterity, because it is the most basic and universal difference of those which exist in all humanity. It is also the place where the first articulation between nature and culture takes place and has to be elaborated, including the relational dimensions which need cultivation towards respect for the other.

Coexistence and communication between two sexuate identities allow us to deal with other differences as far as it is a question of relating between human beings and not of economical problems and power. If domination was not at the root of the relations between man and women, this domination could not act in racial or ethnic relations. The question is always one of domination of the stronger over the weaker based on natural data, at least in part. And this is the symptom of a lack of cultivation of the bridge between nature and culture in all cases. It is because our culture has considered woman as a mere nature that we can stress the naturality of a racial or ethnic difference. But, in every situation, it is also a problem of culture, and of the domination of one culture by an other.

Yes, sexuate difference has an ontological status, but not in a traditional sense. Man and woman are from the very beginning not only two different beings but also two different Beings. They are not a mere animal body by birth; they belong to a different world which has to be recognized and cultivated as such in order for a culture of two subjects to become possible. If an ontological difference otherwise intervenes between two humans, it is in the name of a constructed culture which probably has substituted a single and ideal absolute Being for the two beings and Beings that man and woman represent.

Yes, differences between traditions and cultures, notably but not only at the level of customary law, are constructed through the elaboration of vertical-genealogical and horizontal-marriage or alliance relations between men and women. Their way of dwelling, their language and art bear witness to that. And this common foundation permits us to pass from one culture to an other if we are able to recognize the universal and ontological status of the difference between the sexuate identities.

E.G.: If sexual difference and the encounter between the two sexes marks the most intense and irreducible difference, what does this mean about relations with members of the same sex? I am thinking here not only of homosexuality, sexual encounters between different beings of the same sex, but also of homosocial encounters, those constituting relations between co-workers, between friends, between members of the same team, or members of a group or organization. Is it not the other who is the same sex as I am still radically other to me, unknowable by me, invisible to me, harbouring a secret from me, in just the same way as the sexually different other?

L.I.: I talked about the most basic, universal and irreducible difference, but not about the 'most intense' difference, which presupposes a quantitative evaluation between differences which is not fitting from my standpoint.

The relations with the same sex are always dependent also on the other sex: a child is conceived by the two sexes and our society is formed by the two sexes. Furthermore, our culture is elaborated above all by one sex, but includes the two sexes as polarities of a presumed unique and neutral identity. It is thus never, at least today, a question of relations only with members of one and the same sex, unless at the imaginary level.

You talk about relations between members of the same sex without specifying what sex. Now the relations between men and the relations between women have not the same meaning given that their relational identities are different. And such a relational identity is not extraneous to the duality of the sexes from the very beginning because the relations with the maternal world and one's own body are different for each sex.

It also seems to me that you imagine that it is possible to have relations with others leaving aside one's own sexuate identity. We would be a female or a male body on one hand and a neutral individual on the other hand. This viewpoint is that of Western metaphysics which separates the real and the supra-sensible. But Western metaphysics is constructed by a masculine subject taking into account his own demands and necessities. We have to enter another development of our global being which considers the impact of our sexuate identities at all levels of our beings.

Perhaps it could be the case for you that 'the other who is the same sex' as you 'is still radically other' to you 'in just the same ways as the sexually different other', although this seems to me a very abstract and undifferentiated way of entering into relations with an other. Such a manner of experiencing a meeting with the other does not correspond to my own life, to my own ethics. Meeting an other always corresponds for me to a concrete and particular experience. My attention to the alterity of the other sex certainly is also related to my care about the negative and transcendental. The 'no longer anything of one's own' and 'nothing yet in common' that I stress in the text 'The path towards the other' (in *Beckett after Beckett*, p. 44) can take place between the other who belongs to another sex and myself but not between someone of the same sex and myself. The 'nothing' which takes place between two different sexes opens up to a transcendental horizon while between persons of the same sex the difference(s) are more empirical as far as it/they result from the sexuate identity as such and not from a cultural construction that is not directly based on this identity and even could aim to erase it, for example by a defined transcendence.

I could add that abolishing the sexuate difference in our relations other than sexual strictly speaking is to take away from us the opportunity of elaborating a culture different from our Western metaphysics, that is, a culture that can deal with our sexuate being not only at the bodily level but also at the spiritual level.

E.G.: In many of your writings, from *An Ethics of Sexual Difference* to *Key Writings*, you have indicated that reconfiguring relations between space and time is central for the project of sexual difference. Could you explain why changes in our conceptions of space and time are necessary conditions for the emergence of sexual difference?

L.I.: Dwelling in space and in time does not occur in the same way for the two sexes. It depends on the morphology of the body, on its properties, on the specificities of the relational world of each sex. For example, the fact that the sex of a woman is in part within her body determines a relation to space which differs from that of man: she feels good in internal, intimate and curved spaces, but also in living spaces which evoke touch, and in warm and even dark spaces. Furthermore, the body of woman can welcome the other within itself both during pregnancy and making love, and this opens up a sharing of space and an interlacing between different spaces that are less familiar to man. Woman has also more feeling for permeability of limits, also physiological limits, and takes a greater interest in thresholds between the inside and the outside, notably because of the morphology of her body.

Besides morphology, the relational context in which woman comes into the world also acts upon her perception of space. Generally, woman privileges natural spaces but also spaces which envelop and protect. She feels better in quotidian concrete living spaces than in abstract and constructed spaces. The space that is shared between two women, and firstly of all between the mother and a girl, is not the same as the space shared among men, between a father and a son, a mother and a son.

A further thing: in a culture in which two different subjects exist, who belong to two different worlds, it is necessary to pay attention to the limits of one's own horizon in order to respect the world of the other. It also needs to preserve three spaces: the world of one's own, the world of the other and the space created and shared by the fact of being two. I make some simple and concrete suggestions on this subject in the text 'How Can We Live Together in a Lasting Way?' (in *Key Writings*, pp. 123–41).

I could evoke many other things that are more or less directly connected with space: the privilege of certain colours; style of speaking and of writing, the manner of investing oneself; the way in which the attraction and desire for the other, but also for things, is felt; the mediation(s) or immediacy in the intersubjective relations, etc.

E.G.: And a final question: you have suggested that sexual difference is what is to come, a future trajectory rather than something that has been achieved already. What do you see is the future of sexual difference? What might it look like to have a society, and relations between subjects, in which sexual difference is adequately recognized and represented?

L.I.: Of course, sexual difference has already come – to use your words – but in a manner which obeys instinct: sexual, reproductive, possessive, dominating and so on instinct. Sexual difference has remained at an instinctive level while our mind has been trained for very subtle realities. We have thus become split between an animal body and a mind longing for ideal, absolute, God, without any real unity of our being. Furthermore, most of the time the animal part has been in store for woman and the spiritual or divine part for man. No doubt, sexual difference has still to be cultivated on both sides. It is not a question of only cultivating sexuality as such: our whole identity and subjectivity are sexuated and need a specific development and culture at all levels, and without the reduction of a sex to the pole of nature. The relation between man and woman as two different human beings, each one belonging to a nature and culture of their own, is yet to come.

Such a future of the relations between man and woman, men and women, as two different beings and Beings, could change the becoming of humanity itself, and even the conception of what humanity as such is. Instead of only conceiving humanity in terms of performance, notably in comparison with the animal kingdom, we could think that humanity corresponds to the capability of relating to an other with respect to difference(s) beyond any mere instinctive behaviour. This consideration for a human difference, and not only for a natural or an animal difference, between man and woman could lead us to respect difference(s) in other relations to the other: of a different age, race, tradition, culture and so on. If we succeed in educating our instincts regarding sexual difference, we will no longer meet with problems with other differences because we would have been taught to transform the most basic instincts or drives which intervene in our rejection of different others. An original bridge between nature and culture will prevent us from impulsive reactions regarding any belonging presumed to be only natural.

In the whole of humanity, there exist only men and women. Sharing this basic and universal difference can lead us to global fraternity and sorority which is founded on the consideration for and the development of our own reality, and is not imposed by some moral or religious duties.

Bibliography

Hegel, Friedrich, *Phenomology of Spirit* (trans. A.V. Miller; Oxford: Oxford University Press, 1977).

Irigaray, Luce, *Speculum: Of the Other Woman* (trans. Gillian C. Gill; Ithaca, NY: Cornell University Press, 1985).

—— *This Sex Which is Not One* (trans. Catherine Porter with Carolyn Burke; Ithaca, NY: Cornell University Press, 1985).

—— *An Ethics of Sexual Difference* (trans. Carolyn Burke and Gillian C. Gill; Ithaca, NY and London: Cornell University Press, 1993).

—— *Je, tu, nous: Towards a Culture of Difference* (trans. Alison Martin; London and New York: Routledge, 1993).

—— *Thinking the Difference: For a Peaceful Revolution* (trans. Karin Montin; London and New York: Continuum and Routledge, 1994).

—— *I Love to You: Sketch for a Felicity Within History* (trans. Alison Martin; London and New York: Routledge, 1996).

—— *Democracy Begins Between Two* (trans. Kirsteen Anderson; London and New York: Athlone and Routledge, 2000).

—— *To Be Two* (trans. Monique M. Rhodes and Marco F. Cocito-Monoc; London and New York: Athlone and Routledge, 2000).

—— *Key Writings* (London and New York: Continuum, 2004).

—— 'The Path Towards the Other', in *Beckett after Beckett* (ed. Stan Gontarski and Anthony Uhlmann; Gainesville, FL: University Press of Florida, 2006), pp. 39–51.

New Challenges in Education

Conversation between

Luce Irigaray and Michael Worton

Michael Worton: For several years, we have been discussing a variety of issues, and especially in recent years we have been thinking about the place and role of education in the contemporary and globalized world. Our collaborative work began in 1999 when I was translating Luce Irigaray's article 'Beyond All Judgement, You Are', published that year in the *Journal of the Institute of Romance Studies*. This led later to such partnership work as, in 2003, the bringing to University College London of the exhibition of '*Chi sono io? Chi sei tu?*' (*Who am I? Who are You?*), an exhibition of Italian children's words and drawings with a commentary by Luce Irigaray, and our public discussions about the role of universities on occasion of the Irigaray's talk 'Listening, Thinking, Teaching' during the conference 'In All the World We Are Always Only Two' organized around her work in June 2006, at the University Park of Nottingham. The conversation below is the beginning of a longer collaborative project on education for global citizenship in the modern world.

* * *

MICHAEL WORTON: One of the major challenges facing school education is how to make the teaching of 'citizenship' interesting and relevant to young people. How do you envisage including the raising awareness of the nature and importance of otherness/difference?

LUCE IRIGARAY: In my opinion, the teaching of citizenship cannot remain at the level of a moralistic discourse, as is too often the case. I have often encountered the failure of such teaching with pupils of different ages. For example, in one otherwise very progressive school in Italy, children had been taught to respect foreigners but not the people who were close to them. I therefore heard such statements from the children as: 'I must respect all people, even blacks and Chinese people', but 'I hate my female class-mate' or 'The girls in my class are really stupid'. The moralistic discourse about a citizenship respectful towards otherness has been an abstract, and, one might say, an ideological teaching that has not opened up practical ways of meeting and coexisting in difference, especially with those closest to us. Now, if we cannot recognize, and respect, the otherness of our partner in love, we will not be able to coexist in difference with someone who has another skin colour. It is the education of our instincts, and first of all of our sexual instincts, which allows us to share or not, with every body that is animated by human desire. If we succeed in transforming our instincts into desire, we shall lay the foundations for universal coexistence. There then remains the task of cultivating our desire. We have not – or have not yet – achieved a universal culture of desire, and, in any case, this could not be universal in a neutral or neuter way. We must thus consider and take into account the manner in which instincts and desire have been integrated and organized in each culture. Coexisting with a black person ought to be a question of coexistence between different cultures rather than between different skin colours.

Coexistence between different cultures begins with coexisting with our sexual partner. It is there that coexistence first has to take place and must be taught to young people, in order to prepare them for a global coexistence. As you could observe, coexisting needs to respect both natural belonging and cultural belonging. Perhaps the best way to lead young people to a citizenship which is truly respectful of nature and otherness is to make them aware of themselves and of the other(s) as being both nature and culture. We are natural beings and must live in a natural environment to remain living beings, but our living belonging has to be cultivated in order to coexist in difference with another living being.

M.W.: In your recent work, you increasingly adopt a global perspective. Could you outline what you understand by 'global citizenship' and the role that education can play in fostering this in young people?

L.I.: To build a global citizenship requires us to return to what we share as humans. More and more, we have moved away from our human belonging. We must depart again from it to elaborate a culture which can be shared by all human beings, avoiding all forms of imperialism or further exploitation of humans as such.

Any global citizenship must correspond to our human nature, a nature which is the same for all the human beings on our planet, but one which includes difference within itself: we are man or woman. Men and women need a culture which is appropriate to their own natural belonging. The first component of this culture consists of civil rights, or at least civil rules of coexistence. To emerge from a natural state and coexist as citizens, we must be able to contain our natural instincts or feelings in order to reach a civil behaviour regulated by duties with respect to coexistence. Indeed, such a coexistence could be global if it were based on our nature. If this is not the case, it is because humankind either still remains in a natural state or has lost its natural belonging in an artificial cultural or civic construction, for example, comparing man and woman to a neuter or neutral citizen. In this way, we can no longer coexist as citizens or lay persons at a global level.

In my view, it would be possible to include such considerations in school education. It would be desirable to illustrate them with examples drawn from the culture to which the students belong and from other cultures. This would clarify for pupils both the cause and the nature of the difficulties which we encounter in the elaboration of a global citizenship and would offer ways of overcoming them. It would also be useful to teach them some of the other elements which intervene in the construction of the manner of coexisting in community: key moments in the history of the development of humanity and the role of climate, of geographic context, of natural resources, of the intermingling of civilizations and so on. And it would advisable to explain how these elements can have the potential to cancel out our fundamental belonging to humankind through secondary differences.

Furthermore, it would be fruitful to teach students the dynamic and beneficial aspects of meeting in difference without ever abandoning our fundamental sharing in humankind as women and men. It is possible to make clear to pupils that to stop at one single mode of citizenship or culture is often the result of an inability to go beyond our own habits and customs, an inability which paralyzes both our culture and our own lives and prevents us from taking forward the becoming of humankind, and, especially, our own individual becoming.

M.W.: In 'Towards a sharing of speech' you state that sexual difference is 'the most universal difference, and the one that most profoundly unites nature and culture' (*Key Writings*, p. 84). Could you elaborate on the second clause here and how sexual difference *unites* nature and culture?

L.I.: First of all, I would like to stress that, more and more, I use the term 'sexuate', rather than 'sexual', in order to avoid the all too frequent confusion between sexuate identity and sexual choice. Sexuate identity is more basic and it is more determined by birth than sexual choice. It is determined by both the morphology of the body and the relational environment which goes with this body. So, sexuate identity is the same, or not, as that of the mother; it implies making love either inside or outside one's own body and with a specific relationship with mucous and engendering; it presupposes the possibility or not of engendering within one's self and of engendering or not the same and/or the different within one's self; and it entails a different confrontation with the mystery of one's own origin and so on. Now, all of these bodily properties need an appropriate development and an appropriate culture with regard to one's own becoming and the way in which one relates to and with the other.

Such development and culture are to a great extent still lacking, but in one way or another the necessity of building a fundamental bridge between nature and culture exists in all traditions and cultures. This can be deciphered through the way in which they have been constructed, especially at the level of genealogy and marriages, and also through a lack of or an inappropriate regulation in the weaving of relationships. In any case, the fact that sexuate identity is both connected to the body and a relational context ensures that it is from the beginning both nature and culture, a culture that is, or not, appropriate to one's own nature and that thereby favours or prevents the growth and blossoming of this nature.

Culture cannot be universal in a neutral and undifferentiated way. I know that such universality seems to be the goal that we must reach, especially if we are to succeed in achieving globalization. However, such a conception amounts to an unconscious or cynical cultural imperialism, which causes the loss of cultural identity and chaos, as well as deadly conflicts and wars. The fact that our cultures have leapt over the cultivation and culture of our sexuate identity is probably the root cause of most religious wars, especially those between the monotheistic faiths. We could interpret original sin in this way: the first human couple in our tradition strove to become similar to God instead of, or before, sharing with the sexual human partner. We then enter a sort of madness and exile that has prevented us from moving forward to our human blossoming and a universal sharing.

M.W.: There are many debates about when it is best to teach sex education to young people. However, whatever the decision regarding the timing, whether it be in primary or secondary school, there is rarely a sense of sex education being an ongoing thread throughout education on into further and higher education, even although there are issues arriving at all stages of life. How would you propose organizing the curriculum in this domain?

L.I.: Frequently, sex education is restricted to giving information about sexual organs as the organs of reproduction. This kind of teaching is inspired by the worst interpretation of sexuality in our culture. Furthermore, it damages the sensibility of young people for whom sexuality longs to enter into a relationship instead of acquiring a detailed knowledge of anatomy. I could give many examples about the shame that such education brings to adolescents.

I think that sex education ought to start with desire and love, explaining to the children that desire and love search for intimacy, notably through amorous embraces. It is easy to make this clear to children as well as to adolescents and adults. We must provide them with words and gestures to help them to express their desire for intimacy. If such words and gestures – which correspond to a culture of desire and love – are missing, only violence will be used to enter into sexual relations.

At each stage of the curriculum, it is possible to propose little exercises that aim to cultivate desire and love. The purpose of these is to lead each child to an awareness of his or her own identity and of the difference(s) of this identity with regard to that of the other(s). This can be realized through performing sentences including words such as 'I . . . you', 'I . . . her', 'I . . . him', 'us', 'to love', 'to desire', 'to share', 'with', 'together' and so on. After the sentences have been composed by each pupil, the group reflects on the results and becomes aware of the difference(s) between individuals. It would seem that sexuate difference is the most fundamental difference at the level of syntactic structures and even at the level of the choice of terms, times, spaces and so on. After developing awareness of difference(s), it is appropriate to teach young people how to meet and to share in difference. This too can be realized through linguistic exercises, such as making a written or oral proposal to a friend of the other sex, inviting them to share an activity that can appeal to both parties, or even to invent a dialogue between the two. It is also possible to resort to drawing or drama in order to learn how to meet and share in difference. This can be done at all stages of the curriculum and please people of all ages. I have tried this out in Italy with children, adolescents and also adults, for example, parents or teachers. However, some teachers did not enjoy taking part in such training, because they had been educated to favour so-called neutral behaviour and discourse as a sign of culture. They themselves had been subjected to such teaching in and through 'neutrality' and could not – or did not want to – give it up.

A further point: it is desirable to alternate exercises of sharing in difference with exercises of sharing in sameness in order to train children to have respect for either the same or the other in relation to one's self and to discover the ways in which to achieve this.

M.W.: How would you envisage the curriculum developing in the light of your own thinking of what it is important to include in the curriculum? Or is the notion of the curriculum itself something that you seek to review? If so, could you explain how?

L.I.: I think that the current curriculum lacks training in relational behaviour – with respect to one's self, to the world, to the other. Children are taught as if they were little robots, removed from their relational context. The present curriculum considers things that must be taught, rather than the individuals who are to be educated. Now, an individual is always living in a relational environment and a peculiar world which need to be taken into consideration, and not only by means of a type of instruction that speaks solely to the mind but, rather, through a formation that addresses the whole being in order to lead it gradually from a sensible and particular immediacy to a holistic and general concern. Our current way of teaching results in a split between body and mind within the individual that does not allow the development of the whole being. And this brings about the separation between private life and public life, between natural state and cultured state, and, more generally, it results in a way of relating to and with the other that is either instinctive or abstract, and remains subjected to realities that are already existing and are external to the relationship itself. The individual is somehow lost between these two polarities and can no longer relate to his or her own self, to the world, and to the other in a manner that is both natural and cultivated.

The curriculum ought to consider the pupil or student at each stage of his or her growth and development and provide everyone with a form of education and culture that is appropriate. For example, according to our age, we experience different needs and aspirations with regard to our relations to the self, to the other and to the world. Usually, it is only the degree of competence that is taken into account. Education develops efficiency through competitiveness and segregation. People are led to renounce their relational desire in order to become the best in the group. Education is thus rather similar to a war in which the key question is: how to overcome the other(s), the world and even one's own self?

Another point: our educational system is still based on the requirements of a masculine subjectivity that needs objects, relationships to and with those who are similar, in a group rather than between two individuals; the relationships are also to be vertical and hierarchical more than horizontal and sharing, above all when it is a question of difference. These aspects correspond to the conditions necessary for a man to emerge from the natural and maternal world. They do not yet permit feminine subjectivity to accomplish its own becoming. Indeed they do not correspond to those tendencies that are favoured by feminine subjectivity: relations in two with another subject, a subject who is different and who is generally met in a horizontal, and not a vertical or genealogical, way. The values that are privileged by the feminine subject must enter the educational system as well as the means of meeting in difference.

The diversity of cultures ought also to have a place in the curriculum, not simply to satisfy a mind's curiosity, an interest that is somehow a form of folklore or international tourism, but as an exploration of the various paths that humans can take in order to achieve themselves. The multiplicity of cultures must teach us humility with respect to our own culture, and how to listen to others and meet with them in difference. In my opinion, it is important both to open up to difference between cultures and to discover the basic paradigms upon which each culture is built. Sexuate difference is certainly one of the most crucial paradigms which play a part in the construction of all cultures. For this very reason, sexuate difference must have a decisive role in education.

M.W.: In all countries, one of the major problems is the gap between primary and secondary education and the gap between secondary education and tertiary education. How can our governments and/or schools, colleges and universities bridge these gaps and create a seamless learning and teaching environment?

L.I.: When reading your question, I asked myself: 'Why does a gap exist?' 'What is responsible for this gap?' 'Would a gap exist if education was centred on pupils and not on the subjects or matters to be taught?' On further reflection, I also thought that the gap between nursery, or kindergarten, education and primary education seems much smaller, and, in fact, you do not refer to a gap between these two phases of education. Now, at nursery school one begins to teach what will be taught later in primary school, and this teaching is interwoven with times of play. Perhaps, with regard to subjects to be taught, one could cancel or narrow the gap by teaching some texts at all stages of the curriculum from different perspectives according to the ages of the pupils. It might also be useful to maintain playtimes throughout the curriculum, not only as breaks between lessons, but as in themselves forms of teaching. And these playtimes should be of greater profit if they would favour relational games, especially in difference. Some examples might help here. When I was working on sexuate education in Italy, I changed some sports lessons into playing together in difference. The tensions resulting from a traditional teaching about sports performance and competitiveness were transformed into a joyful relational energy that provided another sort of teaching, a teaching that could evolve deppending on the pupils' own initiatives and according to their different age groups. The same happened in drawing classes and, more generally, in artistic education classes. One could envisage dedicating some times of the week to playing together – with appropriate physical space being made available for this.

To ensure a continuum in education, it should also be possible to plan some relational activities or even classes, in which younger pupils mix with older ones who can supply tutoring aid and help to go from one stage to another of the curriculum. I think that the gap largely results from the fact that the weaving together of relationships by a child in primary school is not continued in secondary school or in other transitions between the stages of the curriculum. And this creates an important difficulty, and even a dereliction, on the part of children who are already moving on to another place and meeting with new subjects to study. I shall continue to reflect on this interesting point.

M.W.: Given that young people are now 'digital babies', in the sense that they grow up using computers, mobile phones, iPods and so on from a very early age, do we need to change the ways in which we teach? If so, how?

L.I.: How will the being and growth of young children be altered by the fact that they more use their fingers from an early age? What change will be brought about by the fact that, very early, children learn something about distance communication by seeing their parents and close acquaintances talking to and exchanging with people who are not present, and then themselves entering into this way of communicating? On the one hand, a part of the body is now more involved than hitherto, but another part is, on the contrary, less engaged. Humanity will become deeply changed by the use of these new technologies. It is often argued that we are moving onwards to ever better communication between us, but I am not wholly certain that this is indeed the case. Perhaps information will circulate more and more quickly, but the exchange of information does not yet amount to interpersonal communication. And it could happen that information becomes itself our current 'object' and that, by being at the service of information, language loses its most human property: being the means to exchange between subjects. Animals, perhaps, are capable of perceiving and processing information better than us, but they do not seem capable of exchanging in difference, unless it is with the aim of copulating. Often this is the case too with human beings, but we can and should do better.

In any case, it is important to recognize that computers, mobile phones and iPods are substituting themselves for communication between us in our physical presence. And it is necessary to counter their expansion by developing relationships between us. Today, many people talk and listen to their computer more than they do with another human being. It should be advisable to include in the curriculum training in dialogue between people, and to draw the pupils' attention to the differences between engaging in conversation with physical presence and doing the same without such presence. It is true that our culture is built on the exploitation, and even the oblivion, of our bodily belonging. Attending to an education of our sensory perceptions would be a good way of counterbalancing the power of technology: our sensory perceptions in the relationships to and with nature, and to and with the other(s). It would also be useful to become aware of the plurality of our perceptions and of the part of invisibility that we must respect in our relations with all living beings, especially, although not only, with human beings.

The reign of technology is based on a logic that aims to reduce living beings to inanimate things, objects, words or concepts that man can master – notably through the *techne* that is *logos* – in order to construct a world parallel to the living and changing world. We must return to our living belonging and take into consideration this belonging, and that of all other living beings, in order to elaborate a culture of life rather than one of death. To give a single example: life does not obey the same rhythms as technology. Life is richer and more complex in its blossoming than technology, which prefers speed, and abstract and fictitious potentialities, a choice that is explained and has been programmed by our Western logic since its very beginning. It is a little disquieting to learn today about the virtual possibilities of technology that attract us outside of ourselves without our questioning the ways in which these virtual possibilities are dependent on our own real possibilities and the means of making them blossom in ourselves and between us as human beings. Education ought to reflect on all of these issues and to develop strategies to counter the subjection of our life and of our entire subjectivity to technology.

M.W.: The internet has great democratizing power in that it makes vast amounts of information freely available. However, much of the information is not validated by any authority, so there is the danger that young people may acquire false information. How can we instil skepticism as well as enthusiasm in teaching via the internet?

L.I.: The internet has a tremendous potential for disseminating information. Before deciding on its democratic power, we should interrogate the nature of the information that is spread. The question, in my opinion, is not only whether information is true or false. This is undoubtedly a real issue, but it seems secondary with respect to that of the origin of information. For example: what culture has input information into programmes and in what language? If one single culture or language is privileged, how can we talk about any democratizing power? Information is already in thrall to political, financial and cultural powers that provide people with the keys to have access to them. How can this be democratic at a global level? Of course, knowing something about these keys also opens up means of opposing to these powers. But who can actually make such a choice, which presupposes the ability to go against the power of money? Will the internet contribute to liberating humanity or to submitting it to some global programme(s) which is, or are, defined and disseminated by certain powers, notably financial powers? And what counter-power can we oppose to this?

One of the greatest dangers that the internet poses is that of the creation of a global opinion, a sort of global cultural and political correctness, through programmes managed by shrewd politicians. In this way, a sort of totalitarianism could be imposed without anyone appearing to be responsible for it: a mere conformism to information spread via the internet would be sufficient. If the internet can open up many people to the complexity of the world, it nonetheless represents the means of manipulating these same people. And the question is not only one of true or false information – in any case who is actually still capable of deciding on this? – but that of the context and the interpretation with which people are provided. In other words, what frames and ways of understanding are determined by the information that is passed on.

Another important point to be considered is the type of encoding, one could say the logic, that is used to communicate information. Not all people are 'compatible' with every sort of presentation and reading of information. The internet can become a new way of colonizing other cultures. The best function of the internet would be to teach differences between cultures and ways of dealing with these differences in order to approach a global democratic culture. What cultural paradigms must be discovered and maintained at a global level? Here we confront the questions: 'What or who is a human being?' 'What is humanity as such?' 'How can we pursue becoming of humanity and make it blossom in our times?'

Furthermore, what will happen to the cultural world, if humanity is considered as two, with a specific culture for each one of these two? Will not this offer the chance of a global democracy? How can we make our way towards it, including via the internet? In fact, the internet can force us to change our conception of education, notably because of an exaggeration of the problematic characteristics of our current system. The internet favours the accumulation of knowledge and know-how without envisaging any modification in the human being that would allow integration of these new data into a comprehensive subjectivity. It is through dialogue(s) with qualitative difference(s) in mind that human subjectivity can reach a new oneness, which is more relational but not deprived of unity.

M.W.: To what extent is education bound up with notions of democracy, however revitalized conceptions of democracy might be?

L.I.: The notion of democracy at work in education is still rather elementary. If all people could, and indeed were obliged to, go to school, this would be enough to ensure that education is truly democratic. Of course, things are not so simple, as I have tried to explain in response to your previous questions. Much depends on the cultural paradigms and logic that regulate education. For example, it is not obvious that to submit girls to a curriculum that is designed for masculine subjectivity is a democratic gesture. The same applies to the issue of the integration of different cultures and traditions into a single and unique curriculum or programme.

A crucial question to be posed is: how to negotiate the relations between equality and difference(s)? To substitute 'equivalence' for 'equality' would already be a creative step forward. However, we do not sufficiently interrogate these notions about their fundamental belonging to Western logic, one extraneous to other cultures, which may, for example, have a different conception of feminine culture in comparison with masculine culture. Furthermore, what would be the meaning of equality between the mother and the child? In fact, we are confronted with the need to rethink what democracy itself means. What use is made today of this word? What was its original meaning? To what extent ought we to talk about democracy with another meaning? Would it be suitable to invent another word?

To return to your previous question: might the real interest of the internet lie in the fact of stressing culture rather than simply economic dimensions, notably with regard to globalization? The issue is, then, how to avoid a simple accumulation and, one might say, a capitalization of pieces of information, that can constitute the most terrifying power. No doubt, a shift in emphasis from money to culture would open up the possibility of rethinking and, indeed, re-founding, democracy. Democracy, henceforth, would focus on the becoming of all humans with respect for their differences rather than on the possession of more or fewer material goods.

However, capitalism can also exist in culture, and this form of capitalism is even more basic and more dangerous than other sorts of capitalism.

Bibliography

Irigaray, Luce, *I Love To You: Sketch for a Felicity within History* (trans. Alison Martin; London and New York: Routledge, 1996).

—— *Chi sono io? Chi sei tu? La chiave per una convivenza universale* (Casalmaggiore: Biblioteca di Casalmaggiore, 1999).

—— *Democracy Begins between Two* (trans. Kirsteen Anderson; London and New York: Continuum, 2000).

—— *Le Partage de la Parole* (Special Lecture series, 4; Oxford: European Humanities Research Centre, University of Oxford/Legenda, 2001).

—— *Key Writings* (London and New York: Continuum, 2004).

—— 'How to Meet in Difference', talk given at the School of Advanced Studies of London on occasion of the exhibition of words and drawings of Italian children in November 2003, in *Luce Irigaray: Teaching* (ed. Luce Irigaray with Mary Green; London and New York: Continuum, 2008).

—— 'Listening, Thinking, Teaching', talk given on occasion of the Conference 'In All the World We Are Always Only Two' (23–25 June 2006) organized by and with Luce Irigaray to conclude three years of international seminars held by her at the University of Nottingham with students doing their PhD on her work, in *Luce Irigaray: Teaching* (ed. Luce Irigaray with Mary Green; London and New York: Continuum, 2008).

Postscript: The Long Path Towards Being a Woman

Conversation between

Luce Irigaray and Birgitte H. Midttun

Birgitte H. Midttun: My first and up to now only meeting with Luce Irigaray took place in Paris during the seminar 'Luce Irigaray and the Future of Sexual Difference' (directed by the Centre for Women and Gender Studies, University of Bergen, Norway, September 2006). My inner picture of this meeting is very much in the spirit of Irigaray and her lifelong work within philosophical thinking. After the seminar we were many younger female academics queuing up at the front of the seminar room, to get a special greeting and a signature in Irigaray's books from herself, the main speaker that day. What was significant on this occasion was that the line hardly moved ahead. We waited and waited, and when there where only a few persons before me in the line, I understood why it didn't move faster. Irigaray showed her awareness towards the participants of the seminar and gave each one of us her attention, and she really used the occasion well, getting to know us all, one at a time, asking about our profession, our language, our country of origin, and our academic subjects.

In my forthcoming book – *Kvinnereisen – 10 møter med feminismens tenkere* (*Woman's Journeys: Meetings with Feminist Thinkers*) – Luce Irigaray definitely gets the last word, and in a way the chance to summarize feminist thinking and theory from the last 30 or 40 years in Europe and the United States. There is a never-ending story here, Irigaray shows us new ways to go on working, thinking, doing and speaking in the name of the new woman *to be*, the woman we shall become.

Reading Irigaray, we will never lose the sight of our origin as women, and neither will we stop asking ourselves, 'What is really a woman?' even though a long and difficult journey will be needed in order to know even parts of that answer, even today.

* * *

BIRGITTE H. MIDTTUN: Is woman still unconscious in our culture today, exiled from her body and her sexuality?

LUCE IRIGARAY: Many women are still unaware of the impact of culture, furthermore of a culture which is inappropriate to them, on their way of experiencing their body and their sexuality. They are divided between a sort of immediate ingenuous feeling and a perception already determined by the tradition in which they are situated.

B.H.M.: The first human being on earth was a man (in the religious sense). Could one say the worst that happened to woman through history is the male domination and representation of the law, the religions and the family patriarchy?

L.I.: Perhaps the worst is that woman has been trapped in a reversal of situation without becoming conscious of this.

B.H.M.: Is the phallocentric and logocentric regime in our culture headed for a fall today?

L.I.: Perhaps phallocentrism and logocentrism will remain a necessity for the constitution of masculine subjectivity until man becomes capable of freeing himself from subjection or confusion with respect to the maternal world. This requires a culture in the feminine to be developed and a duality of subjectivities to be established. Relations in difference to and with a feminine subjectivity can help man to leave the maternal world without denying or appropriating it.

B.H.M.: You claim that the mother–daughter relationship is still undervalued by the patriarchal society, while you write also 'daughter and mother are rivals' (*Speculum*, p. 81). What should be valued in this relationship, and what should not?

L.I.: Patriarchal culture substituted the values of masculine genealogy for those of feminine genealogy. The mother–daughter relation is thus no longer cultivated in a positive way. As women are assessed according to masculine sex and genealogy, they are in competition for the importance that man attaches to them; they are placed in a position to become rivals. To restore the value of feminine genealogy is needed to rediscover a correct mother–daughter relationship. But this does not mean merely to return to a respect for female or feminine genealogies, but to establish a culture which takes into account the two genealogies in which each of us takes place. Of course, this does not yet amount to resolving all the problems in the mother–daughter relationship. It is necessary that each of the two women discovers her feminine identity and does not place herself only in relation to genealogies, but also in horizontal relations with people who do not belong to their genealogies.

B.H.M.: Why are there so many difficult and destructive mother–daughter relationships, especially among intellectual and creative women? You write that it is necessary to give oneself an *I*, in order to become a *she*. Is the relation to the mother one of feminism's greatest challenges?

L.I.: To recover a correct relation with the mother one needs to be faithful to one's own feminine belonging. If women enter a culture in the masculine in order to become 'intellectual and creative women', they will meet with 'difficult and destructive mother–daughter relationships'. But to place herself only in her natural female genealogy is not sufficient for woman to have access to a culture in the feminine, notably because we need a cultural genealogy in the feminine. The greatest challenge for women's liberation is to develop a culture of her own while being faithful to her natural belonging, that is, to become an I_{she} with a cultural world which is suitable for her.

B.H.M.: What is the greatest philosophical difference between the *becoming* of your female subject and that of Simone de Beauvoir?

L.I.: The becoming of the female subject for Simone de Beauvoir seems to amount to subjection to stereotypes relative to its condition in our patriarchal and phallocratic tradition. In contrast to the famous statement of Simone de Beauvoir: I was not born woman but just became woman by submission to socio-cultural stereotypes, my thought is: I was born woman, but I still have to become the woman who I am by birth. In other words: I am a woman by nature but I must develop the culture appropriate to this woman.

B.H.M.: How should we understand your concept of 'becoming a woman' in relation to Julia Kristeva's thoughts on *l'éclosion*, the hatching, of female genius?

L.I.: Becoming a woman is a humble everyday task, which is incumbent on each of us. The '*eclosion*' of feminine genius could both inspire such a work in an intuitive way faithful to oneself and be its continuous outcome. For my part, I often talk about the blossoming of humanity: of man or woman, and in two.

B.H.M.: You state that woman must connect her sexual identity, and thereby her human essence to a horizon beyond herself in order to become a female *I*. What do you, considering this, think of Queer Theory and its thesis of the performative gender, that one becomes a woman in performed instants of language and action?

L.I.: To have a sexuate – and not only sexual – identity is not to have an essence. In a culture of two subjects the notion of 'essence' sounds strange and is not relevant. But, to become a subject, we need to project ourselves into a horizon beyond ourselves, that is, we need transcendence. The one who performs without a transcendental horizon perhaps has not yet reached an autonomous human subjectivity.

B.H.M.: What is the essence of woman?

L.I.: You are talking about women in terms of the traditional Western culture. It is not with the same terms that we can approach what is being – and Being – in the feminine.

B.H.M.: Let us speak of freedom and liberation. In your recent books you write about these concepts within a framework of two or more persons. 'So it is no longer solely a question of our own liberation but of that of the couple, and that of the family in both the narrow and wider sense: political family, cultural family, religious family, for example' (*Democracy Begins between Two*, p. 96).

Has the women's movement and feminism in your opinion been too preoccupied with a political agenda and individual liberation and too little concerned with dialogue and interpersonal relations?

L.I.: There is no doubt that the main tendency was an individual liberation without considering enough the historical and socio-cultural weaving in which woman took place. Reaching freedom and liberation requires a transformation of this weaving. A mere critical gesture does not suffice; it is necessary to construct a new way of relating to and with men. For lack of this, even remaining among women cannot mean freedom and liberation. Furthermore, a socio-cultural world in the feminine needs objective structures, a question to which women are not attentive enough. Now these structures are necessary even at the level of an individual liberation.

B.H.M.: You are interested in civil identity. You emphasize the need for civil rights appropriate to women. Why is it still so hard for women to move from nature to civil life? Can any blame for this be ascribed to woman herself?

L.I.: To have access to a civil identity is the most challenging task for a woman. For her, it means leaving her traditional natural status in order to assume a personal identity. This cannot happen without her being able to renounce dependence and reach autonomy, which always partly amounts to a solitary destiny.

B.H.M.: You write about woman as a slave, and as an object exposed to racism in the Man's world, and within the family. Where do the oppressing family-rearing structures of the bourgeois family still exist today? Do you still stand by your statement that 'Yet, in the family, individual identity is lost; the family is a unity, it constitutes an undifferentiated one in which each male, each female alienates his/her own identity' (*Democracy Begins between Two*, p. 52)?

L.I.: The one who is not provided with rights appropriate to one's own identity is a slave of the established order. Now this is still the case for women. And all the struggles to obtain the right of freely choosing to become, or not become, pregnant is an example of the difficulty of overcoming the slave status of woman. It is true at the level of the State, but also at the level of the family. In order to not be reduced to the status of a slave inside the family, woman needs a civil identity of her own which is guaranteed by rights appropriated to her nature. These rights will allow woman, and also man, to keep their identity instead of forming a sort of undifferentiated family unit where cultivation of a natural belonging is still lacking today.

B.H.M.: Is it a paradox that women today, even many leading feminists within academia, carry their husband's (sur)name? 'The Name of the Father' is also, ironically, central to the naming of women through all times. How strong is the symbolic status of the name of the father today?

L.I.: In my opinion, choosing to take the name of a person whom one loves is more understandable than keeping a name imposed on oneself, because it shows more freedom and initiative. It is a way of prevailing over acceptance of passively perpetuating a name that has been received by birth through imposing one's own choice and decision.

B.H.M.: Why do you think so many modern feminist thinkers seem to struggle with the concept of a female nature (except for Camille Paglia)?

L.I.: Perhaps because they have been reduced to a mere nature in our tradition, and they have not yet discovered and cultivated their natural belonging for themselves. In fact, they adopt the nature–spirit dichotomy of our Western culture. But if this scission can be understood as a stage in the masculine becoming in relation to the maternal world, for woman it signifies self-despising and a rejection of herself.

B.H.M.: You state that 'philosophy dies without air' (*The Forgetting of Air*, p. 5). How can philosophy and thought encompass the bodily and pulsating aspects of human life?

L.I.: But how could philosophy and thought be a real wisdom without taking into consideration these aspects of our life?

B.H.M.: Is it possible to be an intellectual feminist woman in the world of today, and at the same time stand by one's female nature, without being stamped 'individualist' or 'essentialist' in the biological sense?

L.I.: It is not only possible but necessary. The accusations of 'individualism' or 'essentialism' often result from a misunderstanding of the task which is incumbent on woman to reach her autonomy and develop a culture of her own. These accusations are formulated within a culture in the masculine and with its own terms.

B.H.M.: Why does feminist thinking have a problem with the female body and the embodied sexual difference? Will constructivism and anti-essentialism gain more territory in feminist thought, in conjunction with new categories of gender in the future?

L.I.: All the words in '-ism' bear witness to ideological abstraction and misunderstanding of what is the real. I regret that certain women fall from the enclosure of patriarchal tradition to the trap of ideology. This will not bring them freedom, development and happiness. It is not by chance that many young women no longer want to hear about feminism. They try, more or less blindly, to preserve their life, their desire and their happiness.

B.H.M.: What is it about American versus French feminist theory? Are there just national differences, or do we see a protracted and still ongoing struggle to define what a woman is and the conditions for feminist thinking?

L.I.: The differences between American and French feminist theory are perhaps rather cultural. The stage of evolution of culture is not the same in both cases, and each presents different advantages. But I think that it is not so simple and that, either in North America or in France, there is more than a single feminist theory and practice. I would also like to underline that it is fashionable today to stress the differences between women more than the fact that all women share, at least in part, the same condition. I am not sure that this will contribute to help their liberation and socio-cultural growth.

B.H.M.: You hold that we must start by learning to be one in order to manage being two or more, giving as an example The European Union that, as you consider it, challenges the ability to return to ourselves and distancing us from our human identity (cf. 'How to Ensure the Connection Between Natural and Civil Coexistence', in *Key Writings*, p. 224). Can this be realized practically in the world today?

L.I.: Today human identity itself is endangered by many things. It is incumbent on each of us to return to our human self in order to rediscover what it means to be human and to pursue the becoming of humanity. Of course, we have to take into consideration the fact that being human does not amount to being a neuter or neutral individual but to belonging to a sexuate identity. In other words, we have to recognize that humanity is formed by two different identities.

B.H.M.: In your early work you write about the male thought's enclosing of woman and how it constantly adds to 'the death of her love' (see 'The Blind Spot of an Old Dream of Symmetry', in *Speculum*). In your later work, such as in *I Love to You*, however, you propose that man and woman may be together in love, being two, and yet as *one* in a relationship. You also write that one day we'll manage to say ourselves. Has your attitude towards the male and the masculine changed over time in your work?

L.I.: I would need to know the context of the words that you quote to better understand them. What I can already answer is that the first part of my work corresponds to the critic of the monosubjective character of our Western tradition; in the second part, I try to define the necessary mediations to develop a culture in the feminine; in the third part, the part on which I am now working, I seek the means of making possible a coexistence between masculine and feminine subjects without subjection to one another.

B.H.M.: How can we really learn to see *the other*?

L.I.: By beginning with recognizing that the other as other remains invisible to us. Starting from this invisibility, we can cultivate our perceptions and our language while meeting an other, always remaining two: an I and a you who cannot be submitted to one another nor substitute for one another.

B.H.M.: You write that 'we avoid the problem of meeting with the stranger, with the other', and that 'we avoid letting ourselves be moved, questioned, modified, enriched by the other as such' ('Approaching the Other as Other', in *Key Writings*, p. 24). Why do we not want to meet the other as other?

L.I.: Among other things, to spare us the trouble of meeting with our own limits and of losing our usual way of being and dwelling in the world.

B.H.M.: Do you think that it is more difficult for a woman than for a man to be part of a couple or a love relation?

L.I.: If we listen to the discourse of girls, we can imagine that it is easier for a woman. They privilege being in relation, being two, two who are different and are situated in a horizontal relation. Unfortunately, these tendencies of feminine subjectivity are not recognized as values by our culture and are even repressed by education. The aptitudes of the feminine subjectivity for being part of a couple and loving are not developed on the side of women, nor are they valued on the side of men. It is thus understandable that it becomes more difficult for a woman to have part in a couple or in love relations.

B.H.M.: You write about the body's incarnation through words, about sensation and sensibility, and that we lack a culture which is both subjective and intersubjective. What is your new philosophy of the caress?

L.I.: I suggest you should read the text on caress in 'Wedding Between Body and Language', a chapter of *To Be Two*. This will make it clearer than a few words what I propose about caress as an intersubjective gesture, and not the appropriating gesture that we still find in the texts of Jean-Paul Sartre, Maurice Merlau-Ponty and even Emmanuel Levinas talking about sexual relations.

B.H.M.: About the analysis of discourse: you have researched language over many years, in poetry, and in conversation and dialogue with your patients, as experiments between the sexes to establish how sexual difference appears in language and in dialogue. You claim – notably in *To Speak is Never Neutral*, *I Love To You* and *Le partage de la parole* – that language is sexed and speaking is never neuter nor neutral. Is the spoken language between two, in dialogue, the closest we come to the truth about being human?

L.I.: It is necessary to add 'different' to your 'between two'. To dialogue with respect for the different other is certainly a way of overcoming our instincts, not only our sexual instincts but also our instincts of possession, subjection, submission and so on. It is also necessary to understand dialogue in a more extensive way than spoken language. For example, embracing one another can become the place of the most truly human exchange by unifying, through a sort of dialogue, our whole being.

B.H.M.: How can woman express her sexual identity through a symbolic language?

L.I.: This language is still to be discovered starting from a liberation of our consciousness from all its past trainings. Symbolic language first means to respect the other as other, to remain faithful to this other.

B.H.M.: Gender difference and language: does one become more female when writing?

L.I.: It can be a way of discovering a language that better suits one's own identity.

B.H.M.: Where is the true core of a woman's own language?

L.I: Perhaps it is difficult today to answer this question. Woman is still making her way towards a subjectivity of her own. Starting from the many researches that I have carried out on sexuate language, I can say that girls and women prefer relations to another subject, relations between two, relations in difference, horizontal relations and also present and future, concrete and natural environments. These are some features of their language in various countries, cultures and socio-cultural belongings.

B.H.M.: In the book *This Sex Which Is Not One*, we meet among others the lonely and silent woman Alice, who exists 'Behind the screen of representation. In the house or garden' (p. 9). Is there a female I behind the representation, outside the linguistic dialogue, alone in her own room?

L.I.: I only intended to describe the necessity for going through the mirror in order to free oneself from a traditional sort of representation(s).

B.H.M.: Can the spoken language alone create a female subjectivity? A female I?

L.I.: Feminine traditions have often only been oral. But language as such, then, did not prevail, as is the case in Western culture, over other ways of expressing oneself. In these traditions, art was really important as a general means of expression, and also dance and, more generally, gestures. Perhaps they were a manner of writing.

B.H.M.: You speak of the gestures of words that we have to invent (cf., for example, 'When Our Lips Speak Together', in *This Sex Which Is Not One* and also 'Conclusions' in *Dialogues*, p. 209). Has language become too flat and trivial for modern people? How can words really hit home with us?

L.I.: Language has become too abstract and disembodied to say our whole being and to talk to and with the other(s). And with regard to a language in the feminine or between women, it is still largely to be invented.

B.H.M.: Judith Butler claims that all language fundamentally is action. Has Butler remade your lingual and philosophical 'gesture' into something physically performative and spectacular in her theory of gender and identity? How do you generally regard Butlers gender-feminism?

L.I.: I would prefer to talk about this with Judith Butler herself. But I agree that speaking amounts to acting if it is truly performed by a subject in relation to or with another subject or the world. The important thing is to express oneself as a whole being and address oneself to another whole being with a possible reciprocity in mind.

B.H.M.: Are you a poetic philosophical thinker?

L.I.: For me, to write poetry is not a formal exercise, but the means of creating meaning, of making appear, to me and to the other, what I experience of life. In this sense, the one who discovers or defines a new thought has to do with poetry. Poetry will provide the structures thinking needs to emerge and be expressed. Only the one who comments or repeats already existing thought can do without poetry and can stop at an already encoded discourse.

B.H.M.: Do you still write a poem a day?

L.I.: Yes, I do. It is a sort of everyday prayer, as I said.

B.H.M.: What kind of literary genre are your books related to, considering your 'chorus of voices'?

L.I.: Why do you use 'kind' in the singular? When I write as a philosopher, my style is philosophical, and more or less poetical according to the intention of the text. When I write a scientific essay, I adopt another style. And if the aim of the essay is political, I must resort to another kind of discourse. It also happens that I write texts more specifically poetic as *Everyday Prayers* or even *Elemental Passions.*

B.H.M.: Which of your books is your own favourite?

L.I.: I like all of them with differences in the way of loving.

B.H.M.: Is your feminist theory as much a thematic theory as a political theory?

L.I.: It is somehow always the case, but it is more or less conscious. I recognize that it is consciously the case for me.

B.H.M.: In what way are you still active in political feminism?

L.I.: First, trying to define a way of thinking, being, living and speaking appropriate to woman is a political activity. Without thought, what can be or become being active at the political level? I also give talks, notably in political environments and, sometimes, write articles for newspapers or journals. I worked in the European Parliament with an Italian politician to obtain rights for women, young people and foreigners. I carried out important researches on education, in particular in Italy. I organize international seminars with people of all the world who are doing their PhDs on my work. I practice my own way of thinking in any meeting at every moment and so on. Could all that be a 'political feminism' in your opinion?

B.H.M.: In your opinion, what is the most important aspect of feminism for the young woman of today?

L.I.: To learn how to coexist with the other sex without putting oneself or other women down.

B.H.M.: What are your most important projects and topics in the coming years?

L.I.: I do not know all . . . I want to pursue my task, in particular through defining how to be, to communicate and to share as a comprehensive and global human being, without division between body, language, love, thought and so on.

B.H.M.: In her book *Engaging with Irigaray* Naomi Schor calls you Simone de Beauvoir's 'chief successor' ahead of Julia Kristeva and Hélène Cixous. How do you regard such a pronouncement? Are you pleased about it?

L.I.: Perhaps Noemi Schor understood something of my work. Of course this pleases me!

B.H.M.: Are you a cultural prophet, like Margaret Whitford claims in *Luce Irigaray: Philosophy in the Feminine*?

L.I.: It is certainly a tribute from her. But to be a prophet involves, as you know, important risks!

B.H.M.: Are women the best philosophers in the world today?

L.I.: Perhaps potentially, because they have a lot of the real to discover, to make appear and to pass on. They often still lack consciousness, methods and language in the feminine to succeed in this. Furthermore, we do not know all the feminine philosophers of our epoch, and perhaps the best ones are still unknown. Your question also seems to presuppose that being a good, or a best, philosopher could be the privilege of a group or a category of subjects. Instead it requires one to undertake a lonely journey . . .

B.H.M.: Where do you stand on the reception and criticism of your work, in both Europe and the United States?

L.I.: When I wrote *Speculum*, I thought that I would have perhaps four readers. I was surprised by the reception of the book, which no doubt did not happen without repression and exclusion. Henceforth, my work is translated into many languages. I hope that, in this way, it will continue to reach readers capable of understanding it and provide for its future. At the beginning, I was wounded by criticism. Now I have almost stopped reading texts on my work in order to devote myself to pursuing it. Sometimes some oral critiques, which take place after talks that I gave or during conversations, compel me to better explain some points of my thinking. These critiques then amount to questioning and are not destructive.

Bibliography

de Beauvoir, Simone, *The Second Sex* (trans. H.M. Parshley; New York: Vintage Books, 1989 [1949]).

Irigaray, Luce, 'When Our Lips Speak Together', in *Signs, French Feminist Theory* 6/1 (Chicago: University of Chicago Press, 1980), pp. 69–79.

—— *Speculum: Of the Other Woman* (trans. Gillian C. Gill; Ithaca, NY: Cornell University Press, 1985).

—— *This Sex Which is Not One* (trans. Catherine Porter with Carolyn Burke; (Ithaca, NY: Cornell University Press, 1985).

—— *Elemental Passions* (trans. Joanne Collie and Judith Still; London and New York: Continuum and Routledge, 1992).

—— *Sexes and Genealogies* (trans. Gillian C. Gill; Columbia University Press, 1993).

—— *I Love to You: Sketch for a Felicity Within History* (trans. Alison Martin; London and New York: Routledge, 1996).

—— *The Forgetting of Air: In Martin Heidegger* (trans. Mary Beth Mader; Austin and London: University of Texas Press and Continuum, 1999).

—— *To Be Two* (trans. from the Italian, Monique M. Rhodes and Marco F. Cocito-Monoc; London and New York: Athlone and Routledge, 2000).

—— *Democracy Begins between Two* (trans. from the Italian, Kirsteen Anderson; London: The Athlone Press, 2000).

—— *Why Different? A Culture of Two Subjects* (New York: Semiotext(e), 2000).

—— *Le partage de la parole* (Special Lecture series, 4; Oxford: European Humanities Research Centre, University of Oxford/Legenda, 2001).

—— *To Speak is Never Neutral* (trans. Gail Schwab; London and New York: Continuum, 2002).

—— *The Way of Love* (trans. Heidi Bostic and Stephen Pluháček; London and New York: Continuum, 2002).

—— *Dialogues: Around her Work*, special issue of the journal *Paragraph* 25/3 (Edinburgh: Edinburgh University Press, 2002).

—— *Everyday Prayers* (bilingual edn; Paris: Maisonneuve & Larose and University of Nottingham, 2004).

——*Key Writings* (London and New York: Continuum, 2004).

Schor, Noemi, 'Previous engagements: The receptions of Irigaray', in *Engaging with Irigaray: Feminist Philosophy and Modern European Thought* (ed. Carolyn Burke, Naomi Schor and Margaret Whitford; New York: Columbia University Press, 1994), pp. 3–14.

Whitford, Margaret, *Luce Irigaray: Philosophy in the Feminine* (New York: Routledge, 1991).

Contributors

Heidi Bostic is Associate Professor of Romance Languages and Gender Studies in the Department of Humanities, at Michigan Technological University, Houghton, Michigan, USA. She is co-translator, with Stephen Pluháček, of Luce Irigaray's book *The Way of Love.*

Helen A. Fielding is Associate Professor in Philosophy and Women's Studies at the University of Western Ontario, Canada. Her research interests include phenomenology, feminist theory, embodiment and art. She draws upon the works of Luce Irigaray, Maurice Merleau-Ponty, Heidegger and Jean-Luc Nancy in her own publications. She is also a member of the International Merleau-Ponty Circle.

Elizabeth Grosz teaches in the Women's and Gender Studies Department at Rutgers University, New Jersey, USA. She is the author most recently of *The Nick of Time: Politics, Evolution and the Untimely* (2004) and *Time Travels: Feminism, Nature, Power* (2005), books inspired by the writings of Luce Irigaray.

Laine M. Harrington received her PhD from the Graduate Theological Union, Berkeley, CA (2002). Her current publications include an essay in *Paragraph* (2002) and 'La Boca' in *Women's Studies: An Interdisciplinary Journal* (2005). Laine Harrington has also assisted in rereading the English version of introductions to several sections in *Luce Irigaray: Key Writings* (2004). She is a recent Postdoctoral Fellow and Visiting Scholar with the

Beatrice M. Bain Research Group on Women and Gender at the University of California at Berkeley. Her research interests include the works of Luce Irigaray, issues in rhetoric, and the philosophy of religion. Laine Harrington has presented papers at a number of conferences, including Histories of Theory (University of Western Ontario, Canada, 1998); the American Academy of Religion Annual Meeting (Orlando, FL, 1998); International, Intercultural, Intergenerational Dialogues about and with Luce Irigaray (University of Leeds, 2001); Luce Irigaray and 'the Greeks': Genealogies of Re-writing (Columbia University, 2004); Women and the Divine (University of Liverpool, 2005); and In All the World We are Always Only Two: Towards a Culture of Intersubjectivity (University of Nottingham, 2006).

Gillian Howie is Senior Lecturer in Philosophy at the University of Liverpool, UK. She is author of *Deleuze and Spinoza: Aura of Expressionism* (2002), editor of *Critical Quarterly's special issue on Higher Education* (2005), co-editor of *Gender, Teaching and Research* (2003), *Third Wave Feminism* (2004), and *Menstruation* (2005). She is currently editing *Women and the Divine* and working on feminism and dialectical materialism.

Birgitte H. Midttun is a former journalist and book-editor. She is now a writer, and preparing a PhD on Henrik Ibsen's female characters in the light of modern feminist theories. She is working at the Centre for Ibsen Studies, University of Oslo. She has written articles, criticism, essays and interviews for Norwegian magazines, literary journals and newspapers for more than 20 years, and her first book was published in Norway in March 2008. It is a collection of interviews/meetings with ten of the most influential feminist thinkers of the world today. Birgitte H. Midttun lives with her family in Oslo.

Margaret R. Miles is Emerita Professor of Historical Theology, the Graduate Theological Union, Berkeley, CA. Her books include *A Complex Delight: The Secularization of the Breast, 1350–1750* (2007), *The Word Made Flesh: A History of Christian Thought* (2004), *Plotinus on Body and Beauty* (1999), *Seeing and Believing: Religion and Values in the Movies* (1996), *Carnal Knowing: Female Nakedness and Religious Meaning in the Christian West* (1988), and *Image as Insight* (1985). Margaret Miles was Bussey Professor of Theology at the Harvard University Divinity School from 1978 to 1996. She was Dean of the Graduate Theological Union from 1996 until her retirement in 2002. Her research interests include patristics, women's history, gender studies, and Christian art, music and architecture.

Stephen Pluháček teaches philosophy in Department of Humanities, at Michigan Technological University, Houghton, Michigan, USA. He is the translator of Luce Irigaray's book *Between East and West* and co-translator, with Heidi Bostic, of Luce Irigaray's book *The Way of Love.*

Judith Still is Chair of French and Critical Theory at the University of Nottingham. She was seconded to the School of Advance Studies of the University of London to be Director of the Institute of Romance Studies, 2002–2004. She is the author of *Justice and Difference in the Work of Rousseau* (1993), and *Feminine Economies: Thinking against the Market in the Enlightenment and the Late Twentieth Century* (1997). She is the editor of *Men's Bodies* (2003) and also co-editor (with M. Worton) of *Intertextuality* (1990) and *Textuality and Sexuality* (1993) and (with D. Knight) of *Women and Representation* (1995) and (with S. Ribeiro de Oliveira) of *Brazilian Feminism* (1999). She is also an editor of *Paragraph.* She has held a Leverhulme Major Research Fellowship (2002–2007) to pursue research on theories and representation of hospitality in the eighteenth century and the contemporary period.

Michael Stone teaches yoga, and also has a psychotherapy practice. His background is rooted in psychoanalysis, Indian philosophy and the psychological aspects of early Buddhism. He lived in Toronto (Canada) when we discussed the interview.

Andrea Wheeler completed her doctorate at The University of Nottingham in 2005. Her thesis is entitled 'With Place Love Begins: The Philosophy of Luce Irigaray and the Issue of Dwelling'. She has both BA (Hons.) Degree and Graduate Diploma in Architecture, together with an MPhil in Engineering from Oxford Brookes University. She took part in the summer seminar held by Luce Irigaray for PhD students at The University of Nottingham in 2004. She has also assisted Luce Irigaray in the presentation of her exhibition of words and drawings of Italian Children *Chi sono io? Chi sei tu?* (*Who am I? Who are You?*) at University College London, November 2003, and at the University of Nottingham, June 2004. She has been working as a freelance researcher for architects and urban design consultancies since 2002 and is Director of the company White Buffalo Eco-Design. In January 2007 she was awarded a prestigious three year RCUK/ESRC Interdisciplinary Early Career Research Fellowship to explore the design of sustainable schools and sustainable communities at the University of Nottingham.

Michael Worton is Vice-Provost and Fielden Professor of French Language and Literature at University College London. He was chair of the HEFCE/AHRC Expert Group on Research Metrics, and is a member of the HERA/European Science Foundation Steering Committee, 'Building a European Index for the Humanities', a member of UUK/SCOP/HEFCE Measuring and Recording Student Achievement Steering Group, and of the Advisory Board, Clore Leadership Foundation. He is also a Director and Trustee of the Council for Assisting Refugee Academics (CARA). From 1998 to 2006, he was a member of the AHRB/AHRC Council, chairing first the Museums and Galleries Committee and then the Knowledge and Evaluation Committee. Broadly speaking, his research focuses on twentieth- and twenty-first-century literature and on aspects of critical theory, feminism, gender politics, and painting and photography. He has published nine books and more than 60 articles and chapters in books.

Bibliography of Works by Luce Irigaray

Le langage des déments (Approaches to Semiotics, 24; The Hague and Paris: Mouton, 1973).

Speculum. De l'autre femme (Paris: Editions de Minuit, 1974); trans. Gillian C. Gill as *Speculum: Of the Other Woman* (Ithaca, NY: Cornell University Press, 1985).

Ce sexe qui n'en est pas un (Paris: Editions de Minuit, 1977); trans. Catherine Porter with Carolyn Burke as *This Sex Which Is Not One* (Ithaca, NY: Cornell University Press, 1985).

Et l'une ne bouge pas sans autre (Paris: Editions de Minuit, 1979); trans. Helene Wenzel as 'And the One Doesn't Stir Without the Other', in *Signs, French Feminist Theory* 7/1 (1981): 56–59.

Amante marine. De Friedrich Nietzsche (Paris, Editions de Minuit, 1980); trans. Gillian C. Gill as *Marine Lover: Of Friedrich Nietzsche* (New York: Columbia University Press, 1991).

Le corps-à-corps avec la mère (Montréal: Editions de la Pleine Lune, 1981).

Passions élémentaires (Paris: Editions de Minuit, 1982); trans. Joanne Collie and Judith Still as *Elemental Passions* (London and New York: Continuum and Routledge, 1992).

La croyance même (Paris: Editions Galilée, 1983); reprinted in *Sexes et parentés*, pp. 35–65; trans. as 'Belief itself', in *Sexes and Genealogies*, pp. 23–53.

L'oubli de l'air: Chez Martin Heidegger (Paris, Editions de Minuit, 1983); trans. Mary Beth Mader as *The Forgetting of Air: In Martin Heidegger* (Austin and London: University of Texas Press and Continuum, 1999).

Éthique de la différence sexuelle (Paris: Editions de Minuit, 1984); trans. Carolyn Burke and Gillian C. Gill as *An Ethics of Sexual Difference* (Ithaca, NY and London: Cornell University Press and Continuum, 1993).

Parler n'est jamais neutre (Paris: Editions de Minuit, 1985); trans. Gail Schwab as *To Speak is Never Neutral* (London and New York, Continuum, 2002).

Divine women (Sydney: Local Consumption, 1986); trans. Stephen Muecke from 'Femmes divines'; reprinted in *Sexes et parentés*, pp. 67–85; trans. as *Sexes and Genealogies*, pp. 55–72.

Zur Geschlechterdifferenz: Interviews und Vorträge (Wien: Wiener Frauenverlag, 1987).

Sexes et parentés (Paris: Editions de Minuit, 1987); trans. Gillian C. Gill as *Sexes and Genealogies* (New York: Columbia University Press, 1993).

Le sexe linguistique: *Langages* 85 (Paris: Larousse, 1987); editor and contributor; other contributors: J.-J. Goux, E. Koskas, M. Mauxion, M. Mizzau, L. Muraro, H. Rouch and P. Violi.

Il divino concepito da noi: *Inchiesta* 19, 85–86 (Bari: Dedalo, 1989), pp. 1–100; editor and contributor; other contributors: M. Bolli, G. Careri, S. Crippa, R. P. Droit, E. Franco, J.-J. Goux, L. Marin, R. Mortley, A.-C. Mulder, L. Muraro, D. Van Speybroek.

The Irigaray Reader (ed. Margaret Whitford; Oxford and Cambridge: Basil Blackwell, 1991).

Le Temps de la différence. Pour une révolution pacifique (Paris: Libraire Générale française, Livre de poche, 1989); trans Karin Montin as *Thinking the Difference: For a Peaceful Revolution* (London and New York: Continuum and Routledge, 1994).

Sexes et genres à travers les langues, Éléments de communication sexuée (Paris: Grasset, 1990); editor and contributor; other contributors: R. Bers, C. Cacciari, M. Calkins, M. Dempster, P. Ecimovic, P. Galison, M.V. Parmeggiani, K. Stephenson, A. Sulcas, K. Swenson, R. Tyninski and P. Violi; trans Gail Schwab and Katherine Stephenson as *Sexes and Genres Through Languages, Elements of Sexual Communication* (not yet published).

Je, tu, nous. Pour une culture de la différence (Paris: Grasset, 1990); trans. Alison Martin as *Je, tu, nous: Towards a Culture of Difference* (London and New York: Routledge, 1993).

J'aime à toi. Esquisse d'une félicité dans l'Histoire (Paris: Grasset, 1992); trans. Alison Martin as *I Love to You: Sketch for a Felicity Within History* (New York and London: Routledge, 1996).

Genres culturels et interculturels: *Langages* 111 (Paris: Larousse, 1993); editor and contributor; other contributors: M.-T. Beigner, J.-L. Bouguereau, E. Brinkmann to Broxten, A. Bucaille-Euler, E. Casamitjana, S. Crippa, C. Fleig-Hamm, B. Menger, G. Schwab, K. Stephenson and M. Surridge.

Könsskillnadens etik och andra texter, collection of texts with an Introduction; Swed. trans. Christina Angelfors (Stockholm: Brutus Östlings bokförlag, 1994).

La democrazia comincia a due (Torino: Bollati-Boringhieri, 1994); trans. Kirsteen

Anderson as *Democracy Begins between Two* (London and New York: Continuum, 2000).

Le souffle des femmes (Paris: ACGF, 1996) editor and contributor; other contributors: M. Bolli, R. Braidotti, I. Guinée, R. Hablé, C. Heyward, Marie, C. Mortagne, A.-C. Mulder, L. Muraro, M.T. Porcile Santiso, F. Ramond, M.-A. Roy, S. Vegetti Finzi, A. Vincenot, M. Yourcenar, M. de Zanger and A. Zarri.

Être Deux (Paris: Grasset, 1997); trans. by Monique M. Rhodes and Marco F. Cocito-Monoc from the Italian *Essere Due* (Turin: Bollati Boringhieri, 1994) as *To be Two* (London and New York: Athlone and Routledge, 2001).

Progetto di formazione alla cittadinanza per ragazze e ragazzi, per donne e uomini, research report presented to regional authorities of the Emilie Romagne Region, 27 May 1997 (unpublished, but available from the Commission for Parity of the Emilie Romagne Region or from Luce Irigaray).

Le temps du souffle (Rüsselsheim: Christel Göttert Verlag, 1999); trans. Katja van de Rakt, Staci von Boeckman and Luce Irigaray as *The Age of the Breath* (includes also the German and Italian versions of the text; repr. in *Key Writings*, pp. 165–70).

Chi sono io? Chi sei tu? La chiave per una convivenza universale (Casalmaggiore: Biblioteca di Casalmaggiore, 1999).

Entre Orient et Occident. De la singularité à la communauté (Paris: Grasset, 1999); trans. Stephen Pluháček as *Between East and West: From Singularity to Community* (New York: Columbia University Press, 2001).

À deux, nous avons combien d'yeux ? (Rüsselsheim: Christel Göttert Verlag, 2000); trans. Luce Irigaray, Catherine Busson and Jim Mooney as *Being Two, How Many Eyes have We?* (includes also the German and Italian versions of the text).

Why different? A Culture of Two Subjects (New York: Semiotext(e), 2000); interviews with Luce Irigaray by P. Azzolini, H. Bellei, R. Bofiglioli, H. Bostic and S. Pluháček, O. Brun, M. Bungaro, O. Delacour and M. Storti, I. Dominijani, R. P. Droit, F. Iannucci, L. Lilli, M. Marty, M. A. Masino, B. Miorelli, R. Rossanda, P. de Sagazan, C. Valentini, E. Weber; edited by Luce Irigaray and Sylvère Lotringer; trans. Camille Collins, Peter Carravetta, Ben Meyers, Heidi Bostic and Stephen Pluháček from the French or Italian.

Le Partage de la parole (Legenda Special Lecture series, 4; Oxford: Legenda, 2001).

The Way of Love (London and New York: Continuum, 2002); trans. Heidi Bostic and Stephen Pluháček from the French *La Voie de l'amour* (unpublished).

Dialogues: Around Her Work: *Paragraph* 25/3 (Edinburgh: Edinburgh University Press, November 2002); editor and contributor; collection of essays on Irigaray's work by an intergenerational, international range of contributors: C. Bainbridge, H. Bostic, M. J. García Oramas, L. Harrington, M. Joy, K. Kukkola, A.-C. Mulder, S. Pluháček, H. Robinson, J. Still, F. Trani, L. Watkins and A. Wheeler; each paper is followed by questions from L. Irigaray.

Key Writings (ed. Luce Irigaray; London and New York: Continuum, 2004).

Everyday Prayers. Prières quotidiennes (bilingual edn; University of Nottingham and Paris: Maisonneuve & Larose, 2004).

Oltre i propri confini (Milano: Baldini Castoldi Dalai, 2007).

Sharing the World (London and New York: Continuum, 2008).

Luce Irigaray: Teaching (London and New York: Continuum, 2008).

Conversations with S. Pluháček and H. Bostic, J. Still, M. Stone, A. Wheeler, G. Howie, M. R. Miles and L. M. Harrington, H. A. Fielding, E. Grosz, M. Worton, B. H. Midttun (London and New York: Continuum, 2008).

Articles

'Le dernier visage de Pascal', *Revue Nouvelle* (Bruxelles, 1957).

'Inconscient freudien et structures formelles de la poésie', *Revue philosophique de Louvain* 61 (1963): 435–66.

'Un modèle d'analyse structurale de la poésie: A propos d'un ouvrage de Levin', *Logique et analyse* 27 (1964): 168–78.

'Transformation négative et organisation des classes lexicales', with J. Dubois and P. Marcie, *Cahiers de lexicologie* 7/2 (1965): 3–32.

'Approche expérimentale des problèmes intéressant la production de la phrase noyau et ses constituants immédiats', with J. Dubois, *Linguistique française, Le verbe et la phrase*: *Langages* 3 (Paris: Didier Larousse, 1966), pp. 90–125.

'L'inconscio premeditato', *Sigma* 9 (1968): 23–34.

'La psychanalyse comme pratique de l'énonciation', *Le langage et l'homme* 10 (1969): 3–8.

'Où et comment habiter ?' *Cahiers du Grif* 24 (1983): 139–43.

'Une lacune natale', *Le Nouveau Commerce* 62–63 (1985): 39–47; trans. Margaret Whitford as 'A Natal Lacuna', *Women's Art Magazine* 58 (1994): 11–13.

'Égales à qui ?', *Critique* 43 (1987): 420–37; trans. Robert L. Mazzola as 'Equal to Whom?', in *The Essential Difference* (ed. Naomi Schor and Elizabeth Weed; Bloomington, IN: Indiana University Press, 1994), pp. 63–81.

'Sujet de la science, sujet sexué ?', in *Sens et place des connaissances dans la société* (ed. Action Locale Bellevue; Paris: Editions du CNRS, 1987), pp. 95–121.

'L'ordre sexuel du discours', *Le sexe linguistique*: *Langages* 85 (1987): 81–123.

'Questions à Emmanuel Lévinas, Sur la divinité de l'amour', *Critique* 522 (1990): 911–20; trans. Margaret Whitford as 'Questions to Emmanuel Levinas', *The Irigaray Reader* (Oxford: Blackwell, 1991), pp. 178–89.

'Comment nous parler dans l'horizon du Socialisme ?', in *L'idée du socialisme a-t-elle un avenir ?* (ed. J. Bidet and J. Texier; Paris: Puf, 1992), pp. 227–36; trans. by Joanne Collie and Judith Still as 'How can we speak with Socialism on our horizon?', in *Luce Irigaray: Key Writings*, pp. 214–23.

'Une culture à deux sujets', *Apport européen et contribution française à l'égalité des chances entre les filles et les garçons* (Paris: Ministère de l'Éducation nationale et de la culture, 1993), pp. 145–54; trans. by Kirsteen Anderson as 'A two subject culture', in *Democracy Begins Between Two*, pp. 142–55.

'Un horizon futur pour l'art ?', *Compara(i)son: An International Journal of Comparative Literature* (1993): 107–116; trans. Jennifer Wong and Luce Irigaray as 'A future horizon for art?', in *Luce Irigaray: Key Writings*, pp. 103–111.

'Transcendants l'un à l'autre', in *Homme et femme, l'insaisissable différence* (ed. Xavier Lacroix; Paris: Editions du Cerf, 1993, pp. 101–120.

'Importance du genre dans la constitution de la subjectivité et de l'intersubjectivité', *Genres culturels et interculturels: Langages* 111 (1993): 12–23.

'Le lotte delle donne: Dall'uguaglianza alla differenza', *Encyclopedie Europa 1700–1992, Il ventesimosecolo* (Milano: Elekta, 1993), pp. 345–56.

'Ecce mulier?', in *Nietzsche and the Feminine* (bilingual French–English publication; ed. Peter Burgard; University Press of Virginia, 1994), pp. 316–31.

'La voie du féminin', bilingual French–Dutch Catalogue for the exhibition *Le jardin clos de l'âme* (Bruxelles: Palais des Beaux Arts, 1994), pp. 138–64.

'L'identitié femme: Biologie ou conditionnement social?', *Femmes: moitié de la terre, moitié du pouvoir* (ed. Gisèle Halimi; Paris: Gallimard, 1994), pp. 101–108; trans. Kirsteen Anderson as 'Feminine identity: Biology or social conditioning', in *Democracy Begins Between Two*, pp. 30–39.

'Verso una filosofia dell'intersoggettività', *Segni e compresione* 22 (1994): 29–33.

'Homme, femme: les deux "autres"', *Turbulences* 1 (1994): 106–113.

'La question de l'autre', *De l'égalité des sexes* (Paris: CNDP, 1995), pp. 39–47; trans. Kirsteen Anderson as 'The question of the other', in *Democracy Begins Between Two*, pp. 121–41.

'La diferencia sexual come fondamento de la democrazia', *Duoda* 8 (1995): 121–34.

'Pour une convivialité laïque sur le territoire de l'Union Européenne', *Citoyenneté européenne et culture*: *Les Cahiers du symbolisme* 80–81–82 (1995): 197–205.

'Femmes et hommes, une identité relationnelle différente', *La place des femmes, Les enjeux de l'identité et de l'égalité au regard des sciences sociales* (ed. Ephesia; Paris: La Découverte, 1995), pp. 137–42.

'La famille commence à deux', *Panoramiques* (1996): 107–112; trans. Stephen Pluháček as 'The Family begins with two', in *Between East and West*, pp. 105–119.

'La rédemption des femmes', in *Le souffle des femmes* (ed. Luce Irigaray; Paris: ACGF, 1996), pp. 183–208; trans. Jennifer Wong and Jennifer Zillich with Luce Irigaray as 'The redemption of women', in *Key Writings*, pp. 150–64.

'Scrivo per dividere l'invisibile con l'altro', in *Scrivere, vivere, vedere* (ed. Francesca Pasini; Milano: La Tartaruga, 1997), pp. 35–38.

'Sostituire il desiderio per l'altro al bisogno di droghe', *Animazione Sociale* (2000):

12–20, reprinted in *Senza il bacio del Principe* (Modena: Ceis, 2002), pp. 5–25.

'Comment habiter durablement ensemble?', a lecture at the International Architectural Association of London, November 2000; trans. Alison Martin, Maria Bailey and Luce Irigaray as 'How Can We Live Together in a Lasting Way?' in *Luce Irigaray: Key Writings*, pp. 123–33.

'Da *L'Oblio dell'aria* a *Amo a te* e *Essere due*', Introduction to *L'Oblio dell'aria* (Torino: Bollati-Boringhieri, 1994); trans. Heidi Bostic and Stephen Pluháček as 'From *The Forgetting of Air* to *To Be Two*', in *Feminist interpretations of Martin Heidegger* (ed. Nancy Holland and Patricia Huntington; University Park, PA: Pennsylvania State University Press, 2001), pp. 309–15.

'Dipingere l'invisibile', *Segni e Comprensione* 44 (Dec. 2001): 10–16; trans. from the French by Helen Fielding as 'To paint the invisible', *Continental Philosophy Review* 37 (2004): 389–405.

'Why cultivate difference?', in *Dialogues: Around Her Work*: special issue of *Paragraph* 25/3 (Edinburgh: Edinburgh University Press, November 2002), pp. 79–90.

'Being two, how many eyes have we?', in *Dialogues: Around Her Work*, special issue of *Paragraph* 25/3 (Edinburgh: Edinburgh University Press, November 2002), pp. 143–51.

'La transcendance de l'autre', *Autour de l'idolâtrie, Figures actuelles de pouvoir et de domination*, Publication of l'Ecole des sciences philosophiques et religieuses (Bruxelles: University of St Louis, 2003), pp. 43–55; trans. Karen Burke, *Continental Philosophy Review* (forthcoming).

'What other are we talking about', *Legacy of Levinas*: special issue of *Yale French Studies* 104 (2004): 67–81.

'Animal compassion', in *Animal Philosophy* (ed. Matthew Calarco and Peter Atterton; London and New York: Continuum, 2004), pp. 195–201.

'Entering a space and a time in the feminine', in Catalogue of the exhibition *La dona, metamorfosi de la modernita* (ed. Gladys Fabre, Fundation Joan Miró, Barcelona, November 26, 2004 – February 2, 2005), pp. 353–55.

'The path towards the other', *Beckett after Beckett* (ed. Stan Gontarski and Anthony Uhlmann; Gainesville, FL: University Press of Florida, 2006), pp. 39–51.

'How to make feminine self-affection appear', in Catalogue of the exhibition *Two or Three or Something: Maria Lassnig and Liz Larner*, 4 February–7 May 2006 (Graz: Kunsthaus Graz am Landesmuseum Joanneum, 2006), pp. 36–67.

'La démocratie ne peut se passer d'une culture de la différence', *Libido: Sexes, Genres et Dominations*: *Illusio* (2007): 17–28.

'The ecstacy of the between us', in *Intermedialities* (ed. Hank Oosterling and Krysztof Ziarek; Lexington Books, forthcoming), pp. 21–32.

'Between myth and history: The Tragedy of Antigone', to be published by the Oxford Press in the proceedings of the conference *Interrogating Antigone*, Dublin, 6–7 October 2006.

'Towards a Divine in the Feminine', in *Women and the Divine* (ed. Gillian Howie, Palgrave Macmillan), proceedings of the conference which took place at the University of Liverpool, 9–11 June 2005, forthcoming.

'Why is there the other rather than nothing?' trans. Kathleen Hulley and Donald A. Londes in collaboration with Luce Irigaray from the French 'Pourquoi y a-t-il de l'autre et non pas plutôt rien?', to be published by Suny Press, New York, in the proceedings of the conference organized by the Irigaray circle of the University of Stony Brook, 23–24 September 2006.

Index